Voices

9º ano

Língua Estrangeira Moderna - Inglês

Vera Lúcia Rauta

Bacharel em Ciências Econômicas pela Universidade Federal do Paraná.

Pós-Graduada em Pedagogia Escolar e em Ensino de Línguas Estrangeiras Modernas.

Certificado internacional em Língua Inglesa pela Universidade de Cambridge (Inglaterra) e em Língua Francesa pela Universidade de Nancy (França).

Tradutora de livros na área médica.

Coautora de livros didáticos para o Ensino Fundamental e para a Educação de Jovens e Adultos.

Professora de Língua Inglesa e Francesa das redes pública e particular de ensino do estado do Paraná.

1.ª edição
Curitiba, 2012

BASE EDITORIAL

Dados para Catalogação
Bibliotecária responsável: Izabel Cristina de Souza
CRB 9/633 – Curitiba, PR.

R249v Rauta, Vera Lúcia
  Voices : 9º ano : manual do professor / Vera Lúcia Rauta. – Curitiba : Base Editorial, 2012.
  208p. : il. col. ; 28cm. - (Língua estrangeira moderna : inglês ; v.4)

  ISBN : 978-85-7905-933-9 (professor)
  978-85-7905-932-2 (aluno)
  Inclui bibliografia

  1. Língua inglesa (Ensino fundamental) - Estudo e ensino. I. Título. II. Série.

  CDD 21. ed.
  372.6521
  428.24

Voices – 9º ano
Copyright – Vera Lúcia Rauta
2012

Conselho editorial
Mauricio Carvalho
Oralda A. de Souza
Renato Guimarães
Dimitri Vasic

Gerência editorial
Eloiza Jaguelte Silva

Editora
Grenilza Maria Lis Zabot

Editora assistente
Lúcia Chueire Lopes

Coordenação de produção editorial
Marline Meurer Paitra

Assistência de produção
José Cabral Lima Jr.
Rafael Ricardo Silva

Iconografia
Osmarina F. Tosta
Ana Cláudia Dias

Revisão
Caibar Pereira Magalhães Junior
Juliana Bassichetti Martins

Revisão de Língua Inglesa
Nicholas Paul Farmer

Leitura comparativa
Lincoln Cardoso da Silva

Licenciamento de texto
Valquiria Salviato Guariente
Liana Bisolo Warmling

Projeto gráfico e diagramação
Labores Graphici

Ilustrações
Carlos Cesar Salvadori
Ricardo Luiz Enz

Capa
Labores Graphici – Carlos Cesar Salvadori
Fotos (da esquerda para a direita): © Andriy Petrenko/Fotolia.com; © Monkey Business/Fotolia.com; © Arto/Fotolia.com; © Darrin Henry/Fotolia.com; Petrenko Andriy/Shutterstock; © Franz Pfluegl/Fotolia.com; Valeriy Velikov/Shutterstock; Tracy Whiteside/Shutterstock; grafica/Shutterstock; © CandyBox Images/Fotolia.com

Base Editorial Ltda.
Rua Antônio Martin de Araújo, 343 • Jardim Botânico • CEP 80210-050
Tel: (41) 3264-4114 • Fax: (41) 3264-8471 • Curitiba • Paraná
Site: www.baseeditora.com.br • E-mail: baseeditora@baseeditora.com.br

Apresentação

Querido aluno:

Inglês. A língua do mundo. A língua global. A língua internacional.

Quantas vezes você ouviu ou leu essas expressões ultimamente?

O inglês tornou-se uma necessidade básica na sua vida e na vida de todos os que habitam o planeta Terra. E você sabe por quê?

Quando você está viajando e não consegue encontrar o seu hotel, quando é abordado por alguém no estrangeiro, ou por um estrangeiro no Brasil, que pede sua ajuda, verá que o inglês é a língua comum entre os turistas do mundo todo. Você precisará dele para receber os turistas que virão ao Brasil para a Copa do Mundo de 2014 e para as Olimpíadas de 2016.

Se você estuda, precisará do inglês para o vestibular, para uma pós-graduação, para um MBA, um mestrado ou um doutorado.

Se você observar os jornais, poderá verificar quantos anúncios de empregos incluem em suas exigências que os profissionais dominem pelo menos um idioma. E que idioma é esse? O inglês.

O inglês é o meio de comunicação internacional entre países que trocam informações e fecham negócios.

O inglês também nos insere em novas culturas e tradições.

O conhecimento global é produzido em inglês: filmes, inovações tecnológicas, arte, artigos científicos.

O inglês é o idioma da internet que nos possibilita encontrar informações e entrar em contato com pessoas que possivelmente nunca conheceríamos.

Além disso, o inglês permeia boa parte da sua vida cotidiana: nas músicas que você ouve, nos filmes que vê em inglês com legendas em português, nos jogos eletrônicos e da internet, nas redes sociais de que você faz parte.

Aprender o inglês é tudo isso e muito mais.

Por isso, convidamos você para aprender o inglês e abrir um leque de opções infinitas em sua vida. Esta coleção lhe dará a voz necessária para que você se torne um cidadão do mundo globalizado. Mundo esse em que as pessoas trocam experiências, vivem uma realidade mais moderna, mais igualitária e solidária.

Bom trabalho!

A autora.

Contents

Unit	Grammar	Vocabulary	Function
1 The effects of Global Warming on us — Page 6	Review of: Simple Present Simple Past	Global warming Greenhouse effect Greenhouse gases Recycling Songs	Talking about actions in the present and in the past Talking about global warming and the greenhouse effect Talking about recycling Writing songs in English
2 Is the weather changing? — Page 16	Comparative form of the adjectives Superlative form of the adjectives Connectives in contrast: on the other hand, in contrast to Connective that expresses cause and effect: for this reason Adverbs of time used in the Simple Present Imperative	Adjectives Professions Everyday actions Means of communication Weather conditions Letters	Comparing things, places and people Making comparisons using adjectives Talking about natural disasters Comparing weather conditions Writing formal and informal letters
Review Unit 1 (U1 + U2)		Page 26	
3 You must signal when you turn left or right — Page 28	Modal verbs Can Could May Might Must / Have to Should / Ought to	Expressions with take Adjective – forming suffixes Traffic signs Parts of a bicycle	Talking about rules Expressing ability and asking for permission Expressing possibility Expressing obligation and prohibition Making predictions
4 Traveling to the moon will be common — Page 38	Future with will (Affirmative, Negative and Interrogative forms) Adverbs of time used with will	Phrasal verbs: turn on, turn off, call up, throw away, put on, take off, make up, hand in, put away	Making predictions Talking about the future Using phrasal verbs
Review Unit 2 (U3 + U4)		Page 48	

Unit	Grammar	Vocabulary	Function
5 Africa Page 50	Past Progressive Form (Affirmative, Negative and Interrogative forms) Simple Past and Past Progressive	Collocations with feel: feel disappointed, feel scared, feel cold, feel desperate, feel like a stranger Biography	Talking about actions that were in progress at a specific time in the past Using the Simple Past for shorter actions and the Past Progressive for longer actions Using collocations Writing a biography
6 Have you ever been to New Zealand? Page 60	Present Perfect Simple of regular and irregular verbs Short and full answers Ever / never	Experiences: play golf, break a window, listen to a rock concert, have a pet fish, see a UFO, fly in an airplane	Using the Present Perfect to talk about experiences Using ever and never with the Present Perfect

Review Unit 3 (U5 + U6) — Page 70

Unit	Grammar	Vocabulary	Function
7 Brazil, the country of the present Page 72	Present Perfect: Already / yet For / since Question word: How long	Situations using already and yet, for and since	Using the Present Perfect with already and yet Using the Present Perfect with for and since
8 International English Page 82	Relative pronouns Who, where, which, when, whose, that	Friendship: verbs describing what it is to be a friend	Using relative pronouns

Review Unit 4 (U7 + U8) — Page 92

Workbook – Pages 94-117
Projects – Pages 120-123
Glossary – Pages 126-136
Reading is Fun – Pages 140-143

How do you say... in English? Pages 118-119
Grammar Points – Pages 124-125
Listening scripts – Pages 137-139
References – Page 144

This icon indicates related digital content.

UNIT 1
THE EFFECTS OF GLOBAL WARMING ON US

- Review Book 8 – Simple Present – Simple Past – Global Warming

WARM-UP: Do you know what global warming is?
Can you feel the effects of global warming over the planet?
Global warming is raising the Earth's temperature.
Do you know what impact this phenomenon will have on our planet?

Read

1. The students are working on a project called "The effects of global warming on planet Earth". What kind of text is David reading?

GLOBAL WARMING

Global warming means an increase in the planet's average surface temperature and it's causing many changes to the Earth's climate. Glaciers are melting, sea levels are rising and wildlife is in danger. Human beings caused most of the past century's warming by releasing gases called greenhouse gases.

2. The greenhouse effect is a natural phenomenon, but it becomes an environmental issue when the emission of greenhouse gases begins to rise because of human influence. Do you know what the main greenhouse gases are and where they come from?

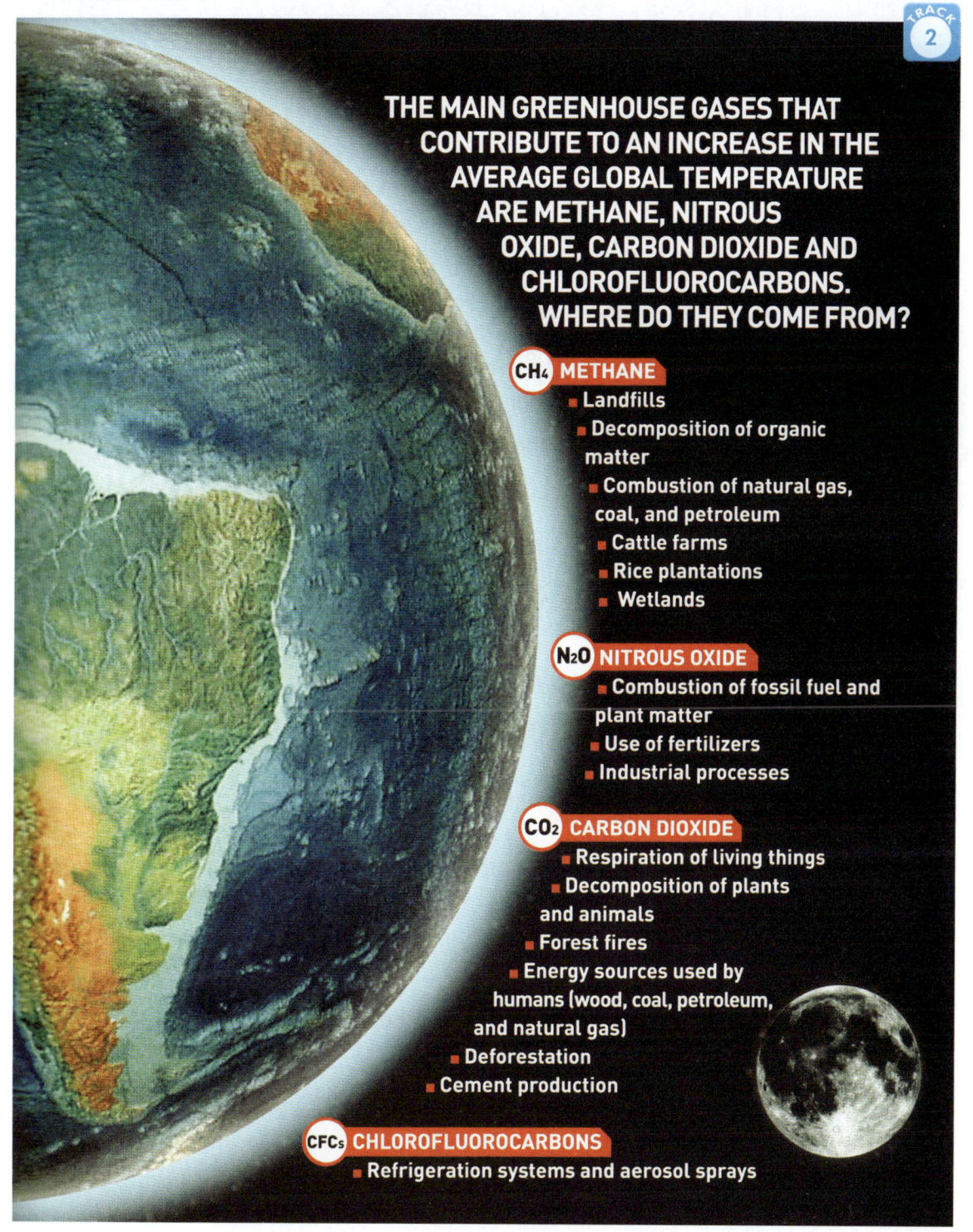

THE MAIN GREENHOUSE GASES THAT CONTRIBUTE TO AN INCREASE IN THE AVERAGE GLOBAL TEMPERATURE ARE METHANE, NITROUS OXIDE, CARBON DIOXIDE AND CHLOROFLUOROCARBONS. WHERE DO THEY COME FROM?

CH_4 METHANE
- Landfills
- Decomposition of organic matter
- Combustion of natural gas, coal, and petroleum
- Cattle farms
- Rice plantations
- Wetlands

N_2O NITROUS OXIDE
- Combustion of fossil fuel and plant matter
- Use of fertilizers
- Industrial processes

CO_2 CARBON DIOXIDE
- Respiration of living things
- Decomposition of plants and animals
- Forest fires
- Energy sources used by humans (wood, coal, petroleum, and natural gas)
- Deforestation
- Cement production

CFCs CHLOROFLUOROCARBONS
- Refrigeration systems and aerosol sprays

From: Learn about global warming, Richmond Publishing.

3. In groups discuss the effects of greenhouse gases on the global temperature.

Listen

1. The students are in the classroom. It's science class now. Mrs. Costa is talking about global warming. Listen to her and her students.

2. Listen and check the words you hear. TRACK 3

   ( ) global warming   ( ) climate

   ( ) temperatures   ( ) gas

   ( ) environment   ( ) polar ice caps

   ( ) Earth   ( ) rainforests

3. Listen again. Are the sentences below True (T) or False (F)?

   a) Mrs. Costa thinks global warming is changing the climate of our planet. (T)

   b) Temperatures aren't getting higher in Ricardo's opinion. ( )

   c) Global warming has effects on the environment. ( )

   d) Sea levels are going to rise because the polar ice caps are melting. ( )

   e) Important towns and cities are going to be flooded. ( )

4. In your group, think of three things you could do to help stop global warming.

   a) _____

   b) _____

   c) _____

5. Listen to the other groups and choose the best two suggestions. Write them here.

   a) _____

   b) _____

Speak

1. How green are you? Try this questionnaire. Answer YES or NO. To be green means to act with environmental responsibility. What about you? Do you ever…?

   a) take your paper, bottles and cans for recycling? _____

   b) take public transportation, walk, ride a bike or do a car pool? _____

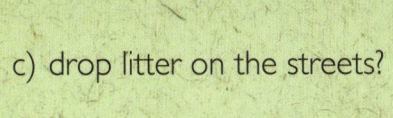

   c) drop litter on the streets? _____

   d) leave the tap on when you are brushing your teeth? _____

   e) leave your computer on when you're not using it? _____

2. Now check your answers. Get 1 point if you said YES to questions **a** and **b**. Get 1 point if you said NO to questions **c**, **d** and **e**. The more points you get, the greener you are.

Don't miss!

Guia Verde Politicamente Incorreto. **Super Interessante**, São Paulo, 9 de dezembro de 2011. Edição 299.

Grammar points

REVIEW OF SIMPLE PRESENT AND SIMPLE PAST

1. Read the sentences below. Complete the sentences.

a) Global warming <u>means</u> an increase in the planet's average surface temperature.

The verb to <u>mean</u> is conjugated in the Simple Present.

Remember that:

We use the Simple Present to talk about habits and facts. For negative sentences and questions we use _____.
Examples: Do you like science fiction movies?
My parents don't speak English.
Does Laura live in a house?
Lyndon doesn't like fish.

b) Human beings <u>caused</u> most of the past century's warming.

The verb to <u>cause</u> is conjugated in the Simple Past.

Remember that:

We use the Simple Past to talk about actions that are finished. For negative sentences and questions we use _____.
Examples: Did you arrive early last night?
She didn't stay in a hotel.
Wildlife is in danger.
The students were at school.

c) Wildlife <u>is</u> in danger.   The students <u>were</u> at school.

The verb <u>to be</u> is in the present and in the past.

Remember that:

We use the appropriate forms of the verb _____ for negative sentences and questions.
Examples: Is Gabriela from Brazil?
They are at home now.
Was Kazuki late for school yesterday?
The students weren't at the library.

Vocabulary

ENVIRONMENTAL ISSUES

1. These words are related to the environment. Read and match them with their corresponding definitions. Write the words.

   > ozone layer   flood   drought   biodiversity
   > ~~greenhouse effect~~   climate   deforestation   carbon emission

2. Then listen and check your answers. 🎵 TRACK 4

   a) The warming effect on Earth: **greenhouse effect.**

   b) The process of clearing forests: _____

   c) An overflow of a body of water especially onto normally dry land: _____

   d) The layer of gases that prevents harmful radiation from the sun from reaching the Earth: _____

   e) The sending out of poisonous gas when engines burn gasoline: _____

   f) A period of dryness especially when prolonged: _____

   g) Biological diversity in an environment as indicated by numbers of different species of plants and animals: _____

   h) The typical weather conditions in a particular area: _____

3. What about you? What environmental issues are you concerned about? Why?

Write

1. There are some songs that deal with the environment and the way we live. Look at part of the following songs.

Mercy Mercy Me (the Ecology)
By Marvin Gaye

Ah, mercy, mercy me,
Ah, things ain't what they used to be, no, no.
Where did all the blue skies go?
Poison is the wind that blows from the north and south and east.

Mercy, mercy me,
Ah, things ain't what they used to be, no, no.
oil wasted on the ocean and upon
our seas fish full of mercury.

Oh, mercy, mercy me,
Ah, things ain't what they used to be, no, no.
Radiation underground and in the sky;
Animals and birds who live near by are dying.

Oh, mercy, mercy me,
Ah, things ain't what they used to be, no, no.
What about this overcrowded land?
How much more abuse from man can she stand?

Click

You can watch the video of this song and check its translation at: <http://letras.terra.com.br/marvin-gaye/72703/traducao.html>. Accessed on March 10th, 2012.

TITLE — **I Want To Live** *(by John Denver)* — **SONGWRITER**

VERSE
There are children raised in sorrow
On a scorched and barren plain
There are children raised beneath a golden sun
There are children of the water
Children of the sand
And they cry out through the universe
Their voices raised as one

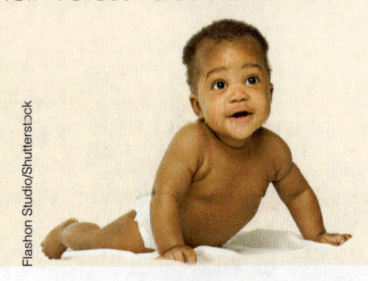

CHORUS
I want to live I want to grow
I want to see I want to know
I want to share what I can give
I want to be I want to live

Click

Você pode assistir ao vídeo dessa música em: <http://letras.terra.com.br/john-denver/169805/>. Acesso em: 8 nov. 2011.

2. What are their messages?

3. When a person writes a song, he or she shows his or her comprehension and creative skills.

WRITING SONGS IN ENGLISH

Here are some hints on how to write a song in English.

Decide which song you're going to compare:

a) The topic of the song can be:
   - Global warming
   - Planet Earth
   - The greenhouse effect
   - Being an environmentalist (when you inform the population about global warming)

b) It's easier to write a song when you're familiar with the vocabulary you're going to talk about. Take notes about your ideas.

c) Songs have a common structure: verses and a chorus.

d) <u>Song lyric's verses</u> contain lines that rhyme. Ballads have longer verses. Some country songs are ballads. Love songs and rock songs have shorter verses.

e) A <u>song's chorus</u> is the part of the song lyric that repeats itself. It comes after a verse. The chorus might be as long as a verse, but it is usually shorter.

f) Verses and the chorus of a song have a rhyme pattern. The rhyme pattern for a song's verse is almost always the same for all verses. The chorus might have a different pattern or the same as the verses.

4. Now it's your turn.

   a) Suppose you have been hired at school to write the lyrics to a song about global warming for a science fair. The song has to teach a lesson. You can write about the greenhouse effect, or how the CO_2 level has increased.

   b) On the day when you're going to sing your song, also design and wear a T-shirt to bring more attention to the issue.

👍 Don't miss! ➡

CAETANO, Mariana; CORDEIRO, Tiago. Dinheiro de fumaça. **Super Interessante**, São Paulo, 9 de dezembro de 2011. Edição 299.
Artigo sobre o mercado de créditos de carbono para diminuir a emissão de gases estufa.
SISTER, Gabriel. **Mercado de carbono e Protocolo de Kyoto**. Rio de Janeiro: Elsevier, 2007.

Let's have fun!

bin types

Complete the words in the trash bins and then match the trash to the corresponding bin.

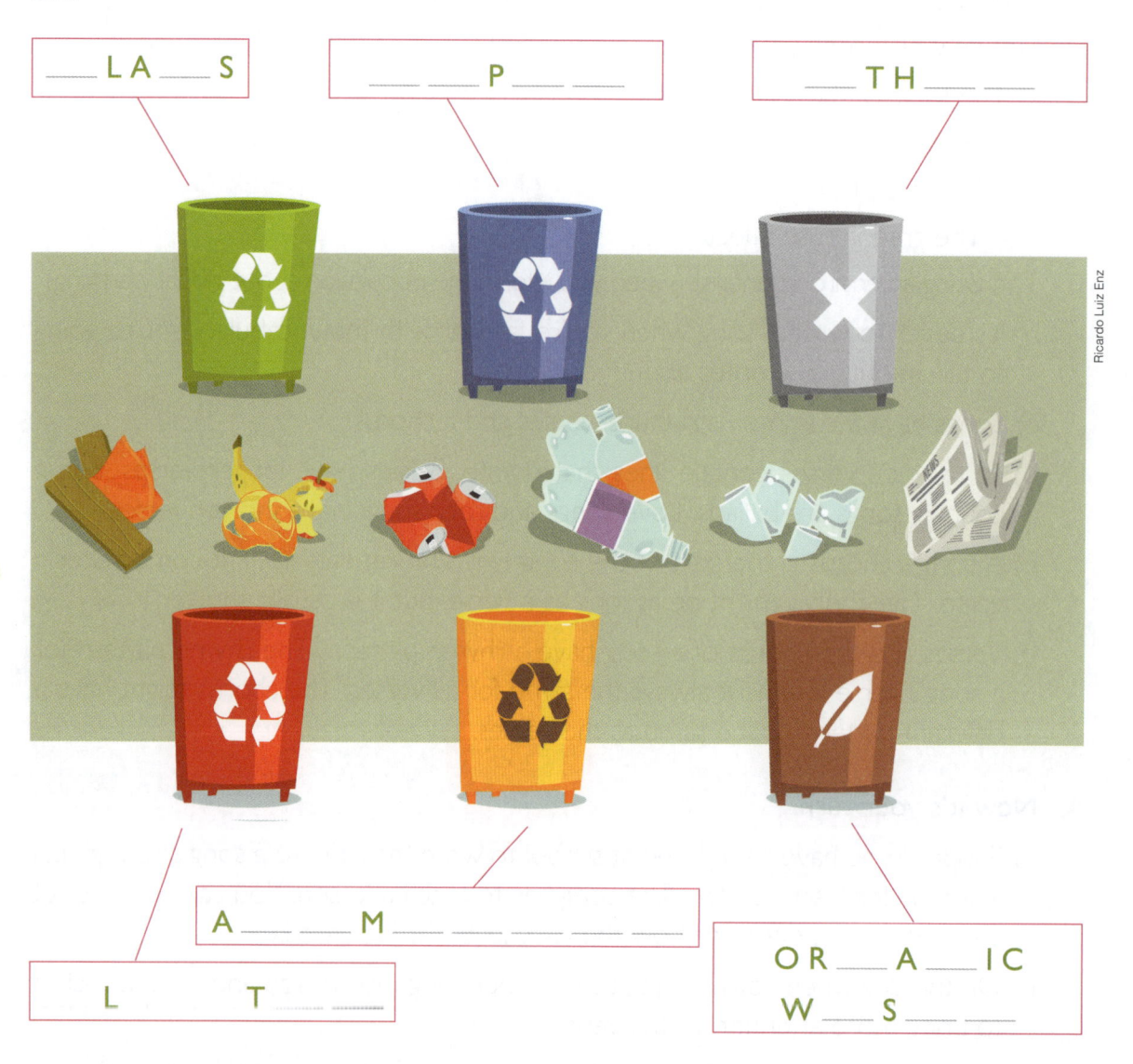

___ LA ___ S   ___ ___ P ___ ___   ___ TH ___ ___

A ___ M ___ ___ ___ ___ ___ ___

L ___ T ___ ___ ___

OR ___ A ___ IC
W ___ S ___ ___ ___

Don't miss!

MITCHELL, H.Q. **Save the Forest**. London: MMPublications, 2011. Christopher descobre que seu lugar preferido, Aylesworth Forest, terá suas árvores cortadas para a construção de prédios. Ele decide que deve fazer alguma coisa para salvar a floresta.

Exercise the mind

WARM UP: There are many ways in which we can help our planet.
What do you do to help reduce global warming?
Are you willing to change some of your habits at home?

YOU CAN START AT HOME!

Each of us can make a big difference. Everybody can contribute to reducing the production of gases that increase the greenhouse effect. Look and see how you can contribute to that:

- Avoid long showers.
- Turn off the lights when you're not in your bedroom.
- Turn off all electrical equipment.
- Ask your parents to replace incandescent light bulbs with fluorescent light bulbs.
- Don't burn trash. Recycle all trash that can be recycled.
- Cover the pan when you're cooking. You can waste less energy and the cooking time is shorter.
- Buy in-season organic fruits.

Now it's your turn.

Work together in groups and rethink your habits. Think about actions similar to these ones on this page that you can apply at school. Make posters and display them in your school.

👍 Don't miss!

O que faz a diferença. **Super Interessante**, São Paulo, 9 de dezembro de 2011. Edição 299. Artigo que mostra como pensar verde.

UNIT 2

IS THE WEATHER CHANGING?

- Comparative and Superlative Forms – Weather changes

WARM-UP: What is the weather like in your city / town?
Is the weather on planet Earth changing?
Are the seasons changing?
Is the weather hotter, rainier or colder?

Read

1. Look at the texts on pages 16 and 17. What are they about?

USA TODAY – FRIDAY, JANUARY 14, 2011 – 9A

World

Body count rises to 368 in Brazilian mudslides

At least 14,000 escape homes, deadly muck

The Associated Press

TERESOPOLIS, Brazil – The power was out, but lightning flashes illuminated the horror as villagers watched neighbors' homes vanish under mud and water. Survivors dug at the earth barehanded Thursday, turning up bodies.

It was a scene of muddy destruction in mountain towns north of Rio, where at least 368 people were killed when torrential rains caused mudslides in the pre-dawn hours Wednesday, burying people as they slept.

In the remote Campo Grande neighborbood of Teresopolis, accessible only by a 5-mile hike through mud-slicked jungle, family members pulled bodies from the muck.

A young boy cried out after his father's body was found: "I want to see my dad!"

Flooding and mudslides are common in Brazil when the summer rains come. This week's slides were among the worst in recent memory. The poor often live in rickety shacks perched on steep hillsides with little or no foundations. But large homes were washed away, too.

"I have friends still lost in all of this mud", said Carlos Eurico, a resident of Campo Grande. "It's all gone. It's all over now. We're putting ourselves in the hands of God".

In the same area, Nilson Martins, 35, held the only thing pulled out alive since the disaster: a pet rabbit.

The hundreds of homes washed away in the neighborhood were turned inside out, their plumbing and electrical wires exposed. Children's clothes littered the ground; cars lay in the thickets upside down.

Buried under a sea of mud: A rain-soaked hillside collapses onto the town of Nova Friburgo, about 75 miles north of Rio de Janeiro. Brazil is grappling with its worst natural disaster in about four decades.

HO/Reuters/Latinstock

Australian flooding

Search for survivors: Crews comb through the wreckage. Little more than bodies were found, and, in one area, a live pet rabbit.

Conceicao Salomao, a doctor coordinating relief efforts at a makeshift refuge inside a gymnasium in central Teresopolis, said about 750 people were staying there Thursday and about 1,000 people had sought treatment in the past day. "The hospitals around here are overflowing. The army and navy are setting up field hospitals to help", she said.

Rio state's Civil Defense department said that about 14,000 people had been driven from their homes.

Nineteen-year-old Geisa Carvalho and her mother were awakened at 3 a.m. Wednesday by a tremendous rumble as tons of muck slid down a sheer granite rock face onto their Teresopolis neighborhood of Caleme.

The power was out, but by lightning flashes they could see the torrent of mud and water rushing just a few feet from their home — and the remnants of their neighbors' houses that were swept far down a hill.

"We were like zombies, covered in mud, in the dark, digging and digging". Carvalho said.

Fonte: USA Today. January 14th, 2011. p. 9A.

Seasonal flooding across eastern Australia has been widespread and devastating this spring – their wettest on record. Cyclone Tasha came along two weeks ago, and dumped even more water on Queensland. Hundreds of thousands of people in an area the size of France and Germany combined are now affected, and at least nine people have been killed so far. Authorities are working to evacuate some communities and airlift supplies to others as the water level is expected to continue rising over the next two days and 38 regions were declared natural disaster areas. Collected here are photos from the recent flooding around Australia and its effect on residents and animals.

Fonte: <http://www.boston.com/bigpicture/2011/01/australian_flooding.html>. Accessed on: Feb. 21st, 2012.

2. Look at the pictures. What do you think the newspaper articles are about? What vocabulary do you expect to find in the articles?

3. Read the headlines. Do you have different ideas about the theme of the articles or the vocabulary in the text now?

4. Now read the articles and answer these questions.

5. Where are the floods? _____

6. What are the key words about the theme of the articles?

🎧 **Listen**

1. Look at the picture below. Guess what Mrs. Costa is talking about.

2. Listen to the conversation and check if the weather is changing or is not changing. Read the sentences and check. (✓) YES or (X) NO.

	YES	NO
It's hotter and it's sunnier.	✓	
Changes in temperature aren't new.		X
The weather is rainier and drier in some parts of the world.		
We still don't know how much it rains over the ocean.		
The ocean is getting higher.		
We can't be sure about what is happening in Antarctica and the Arctic Ocean. It's more difficult to predict.		

Speak

1. Look at the chart and compare the weather forecast.

TODAY'S WEATHER		
CITY	WEATHER	TEMPERATURE IN CENTIGRADES
Acapulco	☀️	25°C
Amsterdam	🌧️💨	8°C
Hong Kong	☁️	20°C
Instanbul	🌧️	13°C
Quebec	🌨️	-5°C
Jerusalem	☀️	23°C
Rio de Janeiro	⛈️	30°C
Lima	☁️	18°C

2. The students are comparing temperatures around the world.

 "It's colder in Quebec than in Amsterdam."

 "It's hotter in Rio de Janeiro than in Acapulco."

3. Now it's your turn. Compare the weather with your partners.

4. In your notebook write sentences about the weather forecast.

19

Grammar points

1. Making comparisons with adjectives.

   Observe how to change adjectives into the comparative and superlative forms. Complete the chart and the rules.

ADJECTIVE	COMPARATIVE	SUPERLATIVE
hot	hotter than	the hottest
cold		
dry		
high		
difficult		
important		
famous		
expensive		

   Remember that:

   - We use the comparative form to compare two people, two things or two places. We add **er** to short adjectives and **more** before long adjectives.
     Pelé is more famous than Ronaldo.
     A car is more expensive than a bicycle.
     Rio de Janeiro is hotter than Porto Alegre.

   - We use the superlative form to compare three or **more** people, things or places. We add **est** to short adjectives and the **most** before long adjectives.
     Pelé is the world's most famous soccer player.
     Ferrari is one of the most expensive cars in the world.
     Rio de Janeiro is one of the hottest cities in Brazil. Porto Alegre is one of the coldest cites in Brazil.

2. Look at comparative and superlative forms of irregular adjectives.

ADJECTIVE	COMPARATIVE	SUPERLATIVE
good	better than	the best
bad	worse than	the worst
far	farther than	the farthest

3. EQUALITY

   Use as + adjective + as to express equality.

   Paris is as beautiful as Buenos Aires.

Vocabulary

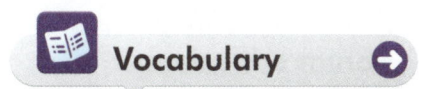

HOW DO YOU KEEP IN TOUCH WITH PEOPLE?

1. Listen to these people. How do they keep in touch?

JULIA AKITA
I always use my webcam to keep in touch with my friends. They think it's better than the phone because they can all see me and I can see them. It's also more interesting.

MAX MARTINEZ
Hi! We use video conferencing at work. It's cheaper than taking a business trip. It's more convenient too. We are always connected to each other.

ELIAS SIMON
Well, I send text messages to my mom and my friends everyday. It's easier and more convenient because sometimes people can't talk on the phone.

TALIA BLANCO
Hello, everybody. I'm a high school student and I usually send e-mails. But I like to write letters as well. I know it's slower than e-mails but letters are more personal. When you use e-mail you get a lot of spam and there isn't anything worse than spam!

2. Listen to them again and check: are the sentences True (T) or False (F)?

a) Julia says that it's more interesting to use webcams when she talks to her friends. (T)

b) Max is a businessman. He thinks using video conferencing is more expensive than buying an airplane ticket. ( )

c) Simon prefers text messaging. Sometimes people can't answer the phone. ( )

d) Talia writes e-mails and letters. In her opinion e-mails are not as personal as letters are. ( )

Click

<http://worldnames.publicprofiler.org/>. Acesso em: 12 nov. 2011.
Site que mapeia a origem de sobrenomes no mundo inteiro e aponta os locais de origem.

Write

1. Do you remember Talia Blanco from the previous page? Look at the letter she wrote to a college asking for general information.

Why learn?

Writing a formal letter:
A formal letter is more formal than a friendly letter. This means that it sounds polite and businesslike. When you write a formal letter check the content, spelling and grammar carefully. If necessary, write it again. The way you write a letter may help you decide your future.

This is your address. Do not include your name in it. → Piazza della Rovere 276
Rome, Italy

This is the date. → May 25th, 2012

Full address of the person to whom you are writing to. → Dr. Louise Smith
Admissions Office
Management Building, Room 242
University of New York 70
Washington Square South New York, NY 10012 USA

Greeting: Use Dear Sir/Dear Madam in case you do not know the name of the person you are writing to. The greeting is followed by a comma. → Dear Ms. Smith,

My name is Talia Blanco I am a high school student from Venice, Italy and I am going to graduate in June of this year. I plan to start college next year and major in History. I found some general information about your university and I felt motivated by the quality of the History Department. Another reason is the fact that I would like to enlarge my cultural awareness by studying at a foreign university and in my opinion, your institution is this right place for me.

Remember not to use informal language like contractions.

For this reason I am writing to request information about your graduation program. I would be very thankful if you could send me an application form and other information you consider might be important for international students like me.

Thank you very much for your attention. I am looking forward to hearing from you soon.

The closing is the farewell. It's followed by a comma. → Sincerely yours,

It's Talia's printed name. → Talia Blanco

- Paragraphs are separated by blank lines.
- 1st paragraph: The purpose of Talia's letter: to request something.
- She writes about her and gives brief information.
- She lists the reasons for writing.
- 2nd paragraph: Talia states what action she expects from Ms. Smith: to send her information.
- She's respectful!
- This is the last paragraph.

Why learn?

Writing an informal letter:
A friendly letter may be written to share news, to give help and encouragement, to give or accept invitation, or to thank someone for his/her gift or hospitality.

2. Now Talia is writing another letter. It's for her friend Lisa Thompson who lives in New York, USA. Copy the parts of her letter in the corresponding spaces.

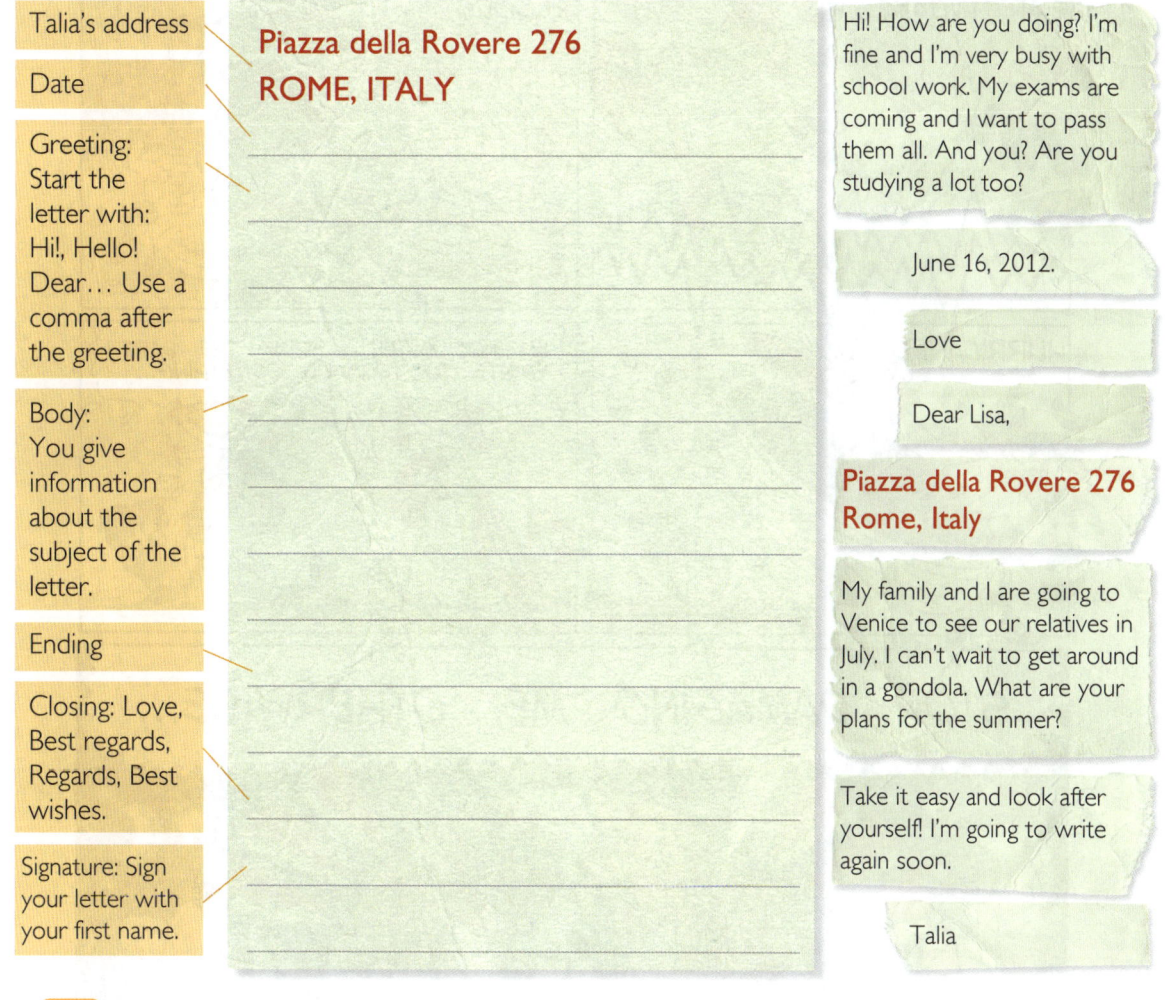

Talia's address	**Piazza della Rovere 276** **ROME, ITALY**
Date	
Greeting: Start the letter with: Hi!, Hello! Dear… Use a comma after the greeting.	
Body: You give information about the subject of the letter.	
Ending	
Closing: Love, Best regards, Regards, Best wishes.	
Signature: Sign your letter with your first name.	

Scrambled parts of Talia's letter:

- Hi! How are you doing? I'm fine and I'm very busy with school work. My exams are coming and I want to pass them all. And you? Are you studying a lot too?
- June 16, 2012.
- Love
- Dear Lisa,
- **Piazza della Rovere 276**
 Rome, Italy
- My family and I are going to Venice to see our relatives in July. I can't wait to get around in a gondola. What are your plans for the summer?
- Take it easy and look after yourself! I'm going to write again soon.
- Talia

Remember that:

When writing an informal letter:
- Use contractions
- Use abbreviations
- Use simple and short sentences
- Could use slang
- Could use exclamation marks.

3. Now it's your turn. Suppose you're Lisa. Answer Talia's letter. Use the parts of the letter in exercise 2 as a reference to your writing.

23

Let's have fun!

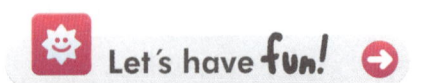

1. Read the comics. What are other natural disasters?

VAPT e VUPT POR MARCIO

EARTHQUAKES

FLOODS

HURRICANES

I'M NOT SURE! I THINK THE EARTH WANTS TO TELL US SOMETHING...

STOP DAMAGING ME, OTHERWISE...

www.marciobaraldi.com.br

2. In your opinion, what does the Earth mean when it says "Stop damaging me, otherwise…"? Share your opinion with your classmates.

Exercise the mind

DID YOU KNOW THAT?

YAN DEFEN (on the right of the photo) is from China. She recorded an average height of 2.33 m when last documented. There is evidence that suggests Defen may still be growing, as a portion of tumor remains on her pituitary gland, the organ that regulates the production of growth hormone. She is currently too ill to be remeasured.

from: <www.guinnessworldrecords.com/records/tallest-woman—living->. Accessed on: Nov. 12th, 2011.

OTHER WORLD RECORDS YOU MAY NOT KNOW:

- Longest fingernails (female) ever. The longest fingernails belonged to Lee Redmond (USA) who started to grow them in 1979 and reached 8.65 m (Madrid, Spain, 2008). She lost her nails in a car accident in 2009.

   From: <www.guinnessworldrecords.com/longest-fingernails-(female)-ever>. Accessed on: Nov. 12th, 2011

- The most consecutive association football victories across all competitions was 24 by Coritiba Football Club from Curitiba, Brazil between 3rd February and 5th May 2011.

   From: <http://footballfashion.org/wordpress/2011/10/16/coritiba-foot-ball-club-lotto-2011-third-kit-camisa/>. Accessed on: Nov. 12th, 2011.

- Maria Gomes Valentim was listed by the Guinness World Records as the world's oldest person. She died on June 21st, 2011, just some weeks before her 115th, birthday.

   From: <http://abcnews.go.com/technology/wireStory?id=13894033>. Accessed on: Nov. 12th, 2011.

Click

<www.guinnessworldrecords.com>. Acesso em: 12 nov. 2011.

Página do *Guinness World Records* que é uma edição publicada anualmente e que contém uma coleção de recordes reconhecidos internacionalmente, nas áreas científicas, tecnológicas e comportamentais da humanidade.

Review 1: UNIT 1/2

1. Read the texts.

This is the Amazon Forest. It's a rainforest. There were many trees in the Amazon rainforest in the past. Nowadays it is facing deforestation and environmental problems. Farming practices led to deforestation and caused extensive environmental damage.

There are lots of beautiful beaches in Asia. Lots of tourists visit them every year. But in December 2004 a tsunami reached Asia. Indonesia was the hardest hit, followed by Sri Lanka, India and Thailand. The worldwide community donated billions of dollars in humanitarian aid.

2. Read both texts again and:
   – Underline the regular verbs in the past
   – Circle the irregular verbs in the past

3. Copy sentences with the verb "there to be" in the corresponding column.

Present	Past

4. Put the verbs from the text in the present and in the past form.

INFINITIVE	PRESENT	PAST FORM
be		
face		
lead		
cause		
visit		
reach		
follow		
donate		

26

5. Complete the sentences with the comparative form of the adjectives.

a) Webcam calls are **nicer** than phone calls. (nice)

b) E-cards are _____ to open than real cards. (hard)

c) E-mails aren't _____ than regular mail. (expensive)

d) Cellphone calls aren't _____ than regular calls. (cheap)

e) Text messages are _____ than phone calls. (fun)

f) E-mail is good, but instant messaging is _____. (good)

g) It's _____ to write letters than e-mails. (convenient)

6. Complete the questions. Write the superlative form of the adjectives in parentheses. Talk to your classmates.

		ME	CLASSMATE
a)	The **fastest** (fast) car I know is...		
b)	The _____ (difficult) subject I study is...		
c)	The _____ (good) male singer I know is...		
d)	The _____ (bad) chore I have to do is...		
e)	The _____ (beautiful) Brazilian actress is...		
f)	The _____ (boring) TV commercial is...		
g)	The _____ (busy) day at school is...		
h)	The _____ (old) person in my family is...		
i)	The _____ (far) supermarket from my house is...		

UNIT 3

YOU MUST SIGNAL WHEN YOU TURN LEFT OR RIGHT

- Modals – Expressions with take – Phrasal verbs – Talking about bullying

WARM-UP: Which of these traffic signs are in your neighborhood?
What other traffic signs do you usually see?
Do pedestrians have the right-of-way (the right to go first) in your city?

Read

1. Look at the signs and match.

( ) Traffic in a single direction
( ) Bicycle lane
( ) Do not enter
( ) You must stop before proceeding

( ) Wild animals
( ) Men working
(1) Children crossing
( ) Right-of-way on busy roads

2. Describe the differences between traffic signs in different countries.

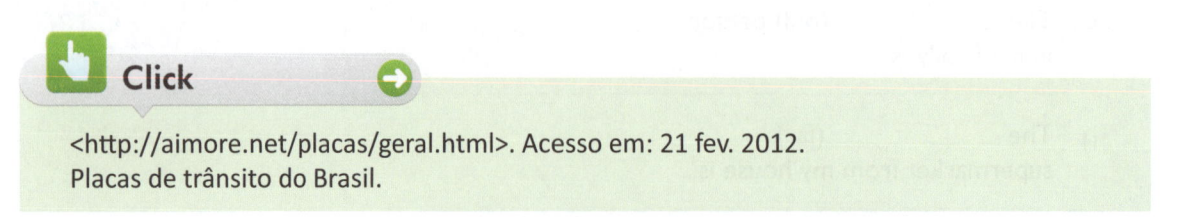

Click

<http://aimore.net/placas/geral.html>. Acesso em: 21 fev. 2012.
Placas de trânsito do Brasil.

3. Do you have a bike? Where do you ride your bike?

BIKE SAFETY

Riding a bike is a really exciting activity. You can join your friends, you can go to places that are too far to walk, you can go on bike rides, but before driving your parents crazy about it, remember that:

- You must obey traffic signs and traffic lights;
- Riding against traffic can have you open to collisions. Always ride your bike in bicycle lanes; If there aren't any bike lanes in your city, ride your bicycle the same directions of the cars.
- When you ride your bike it may be hard for cars and other vehicles to see you easily. You should wear bright colors during the day;
- You must signal when you turn left or right;
- Bikes can be dangerous. You must wear a bike helmet to protect your head.
- Be alert when riding and listening to music. If it stops you from hearing things such as pedestrians, traffic and horns turn it down and ride without your earphones.
- Bike tricks or riding your bike without your hands are dangerous and should not be done. Always ride your bike with both hands on the wheel.

4. Look at these two cycles. What's the difference?

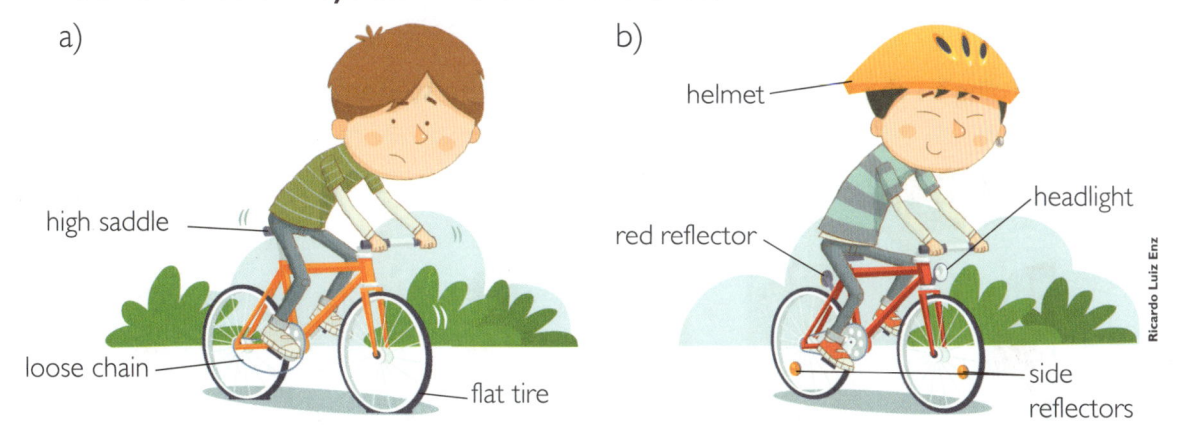

a) high saddle, loose chain, flat tire

b) helmet, red reflector, headlight, side reflectors

Cyclist a is not wearing a helmet. His saddle is high, both tires are flat and the chain is loose.

Cyclist b _____

Listen

1. Listen to the monologue. What's going on?

Traffic officer: Hi, my name's Paula Lima. You can call me Paula. I'm here today to remind you about how very simple attitudes may prevent pedestrians from having accidents. So, before you cross a street, you should always:

- Look for cars;
- Choose the safest routes to walk with the fewest and safest streets to cross;
- Use sidewalks. If there aren't any sidewalks, walk as far from the cars as possible;
- Cross at signalized intersections whenever possible;
- Remember to walk. Do not run across the street;
- Look left, right and left and then cross the street;
- Finally, if you cross between parked cars, stop at the curb and check to see if the cars are running or if anyone is in the driver's seat.

2. According to the traffic officer, what should the students not do? Cross out the picture.

a) b) c)

Click

Site com um dicionário português/inglês com termos de trânsito.
<www.sinaldetransito.com.br/dicionario-portugues-ingles.php>. Acesso em: 14 nov. 2011.

Speak

1. Look at the sentences below. Copy the sentences in the corresponding spaces.

   You should take your umbrella.   ~~You don't have to pay. It's free.~~

   You can't swim here.   You mustn't smoke here.

   Mrs. Costa could ride a bike when she was 6 years old.

   You can go home at 11:00 a.m.

   a) **FREE CONCERT TONIGHT AT 7:00 p.m. GALAXY THEATER**

   You don't have to pay. It's free.

   b) _____

   c) ENGLISH CLASS TUESDAYS AND THURSDAYS FROM 9:00 TO 11:00 a.m.
   _____

   d) _____

   e) NO SWIMMING
   _____

   f) WEATHER FORECAST
   _____

2. What about you? Talk to your classmates about:

   EX: **I don't have to walk the dog.**

   - One thing you don't have to do at home: _____
   - One thing you mustn't do at school: _____
   - One thing you can do at school: _____
   - One thing you could do when you were a child: _____
   - One thing you can't do in a public place: _____
   - One thing you should do before the test: _____

31

Grammar points

1. You should know the modals used in each situation. You should also know what kind of sentences are used in each situation. For example, in the sentence:

   You <u>must</u> signal when you turn left or right.

   must = necessity

Remember that:

Modal verbs tell us whether something is good, bad, not allowed, possible impossible, etc. Look at the chart below.

2. Look at the chart below. Listen to the examples. TRACK 8

MODAL VERB	USE	EXAMPLE
CAN	Ability in the present; request; permission	She can speak Chinese. / Can I ask you a favor? / You can come in now.
COULD	Ability in the past; request; suggestion	She could speak Chinese when she was 10. / Could I ask you a favor? / We could go to the circus.
MAY	Permission Possibility in the present	May I come in? He may arrive tomorrow.
MIGHT	Remote possibility	It might rain today.
MUST / HAVE TO	Obligation	I must leave now. I have to go now.
MUSTN'T	Prohibition	You mustn't use your cellphone in the classroom.
SHOULD	Advice; moral obligation	You should stop smoking. We should respect our planet.
OUGHT TO	Similar to *should*, but not usually used in questions or negative sentences. Use *should* instead.	You ought to read that book. It's very interesting.

3. Now go back to page 30 exercise 1. In your notebook copy the sentences with the modal verbs and their use.

   Example: You can call me Paula (can = permission).

Vocabulary

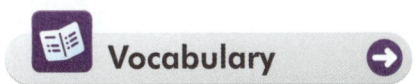

1. Look at some expressions with <u>take</u>. Listen to the expressions. Read the sentences. **TRACK 9**

a) "It takes time to learn English. You need to study hard."
TAKE TIME

b) "Dad, you're working too much. Take a break now!"

c) "Cate, take a look at my new cellphone. It's cool!"

d) "I'm going to take a trip to Rome on my vacation."

e) "Mom! I'm going to take a shower, ok?"

f) "What do I like most on Sundays? I can take a nap."

g) "Next year I'm going to take an Italian course." "That's a good idea!"

h) "Let's take a taxi to go to the airport."

i) "Ok, let's take the test. Good luck?" "Thank you. You too."

33

Write

1. Look at the sentences below from the text on page 29.

   > Bikes can be dangerous. You must wear a bike helmet to protect your head.

2. In the sentence "Bikes can be dangerous", what role does <u>dangerous</u> play within the sentences?

   _____

3. Adjectives answer certain questions according to their place within sentences. In the sentences above the question is: What can bikes be like?

   _____

4. Adjectives come often immediately before nouns or pronouns they modify. In the sentence "Bikes can be dangerous", the adjective "dangerous" comes after the linking verb _____.

   In this case the adjective describes the subject.

5. How are adjectives formed? Learn how to recognize some common adjective endings (adjective-forming suffixes). Look at the lists below, use the dictionary and with your teacher's help try to find three more adjectives with the corresponding ending.

   -able

available	valuable	movable
dependable	_____	_____

   -ible

edible	divisible	credible
_____	_____	_____

   -ary / -ory

revolutionary	sedentary	predatory
_____	_____	_____

| ar- |

familiar · irregular · particular

| -ant / -ent |

abundant · brilliant · ignorant

| -ful |

useful · careful · youthful

| -ous |

furious · dangerous · superstitious

> **Click**
>
> <http://grammar.about.com/od/words/a/comsuffixes.htm>. Acesso em: 21 fev. 2012.
> <http://www.grammar-quizzes.com/adj-forms.html>. Acesso em: 21 fev. 2012.
> *Sites* com exemplos de sufixos formados a partir de adjetivos.

6. Let's play a game of alphabetical adjectives in pairs. You need a dictionary to play this game.
   a) To play this game, choose a letter to be the first letter of a noun. For example: **t**
   b) Then make a list with nouns that start with t. You must not repeat the noun. Ex: tiger, table, tennis, etc.
   c) Make a list with adjectives in alphabetical order: Ex.: auditory, brilliant, careful, divisible, etc….
   d) The first one to finish is the winner.
   e) Try to use the adjectives from pages 34 and 35 in your list. But you can also include new adjectives.

Example:

auditory tiger, brilliant teacher, careful tailor, divisible table, edible tomato, etc…

Let's have fun!

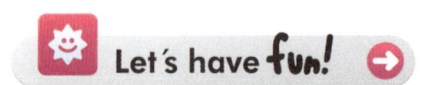

Match the words to the signs. Play the game and say the commands.

the traffic signs game

- TURN LEFT
- PARK HERE
- STOP
- DO NOT STOP
- START
- MEN WORKING
- GO
- ONE WAY
- PEDESTRIAN CROSSING
- TURN RIGHT
- GIVING WAY
- FINISH

36

Exercise the mind

In Portuguese it means "intimidar" or "atormentar".

WARM-UP: Do you know what bullying is?

Why does bullying happen?

What are the effects it can have on people?

Who are the bullies? (a bully is a person who tries to hurt others by making them feel uncomfortable.)

1. Think about a definition for this word.
2. Think about key words when talking about bullying.
3. What are the main types of bullying?
4. Draw a mind map about <u>bullying</u>.

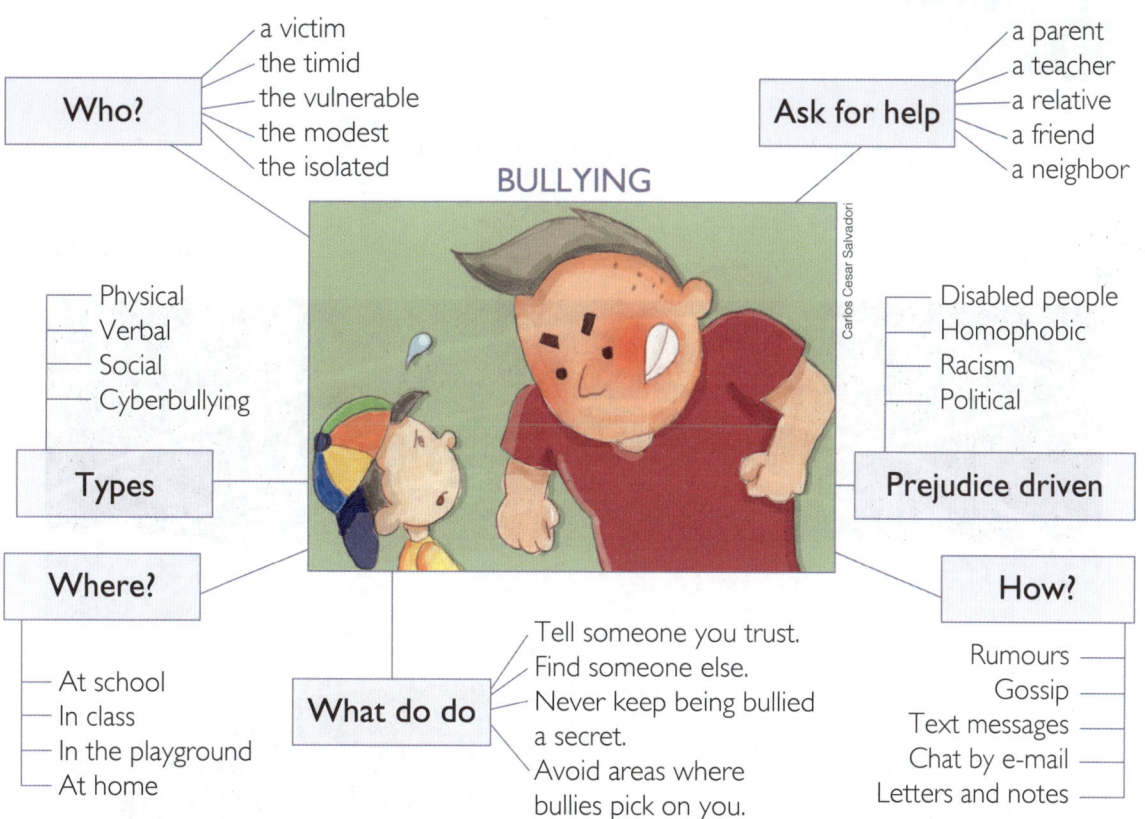

Who?
- a victim
- the timid
- the vulnerable
- the modest
- the isolated

Ask for help
- a parent
- a teacher
- a relative
- a friend
- a neighbor

BULLYING

Types
- Physical
- Verbal
- Social
- Cyberbullying

Prejudice driven
- Disabled people
- Homophobic
- Racism
- Political

Where?
- At school
- In class
- In the playground
- At home

What do do
- Tell someone you trust.
- Find someone else.
- Never keep being bullied a secret.
- Avoid areas where bullies pick on you.

How?
- Rumours
- Gossip
- Text messages
- Chat by e-mail
- Letters and notes

5. What can you do to stop bullying in your school? Write sentences.

SOMEONE IS BULLYING YOU:	SOMEONE YOU KNOW IS BEING BULLIED:
You must tell someone you trust about it. Try to surround yourself with friends and people who will stand up for you.	Get together with your friend and talk to the bully. He / She must know this is not accepted in your school.

37

UNIT 4
TRAVELING TO THE MOON WILL BE COMMON

- Will – Making predictions – Talking about the future – Using phrasal verbs

WARM-UP: Do you think you will ever travel to space?
Will you ever be able to live in the Moon?
Would you like to live on the Moon?

Read

1. Look at the picture below. What kind of text is it?

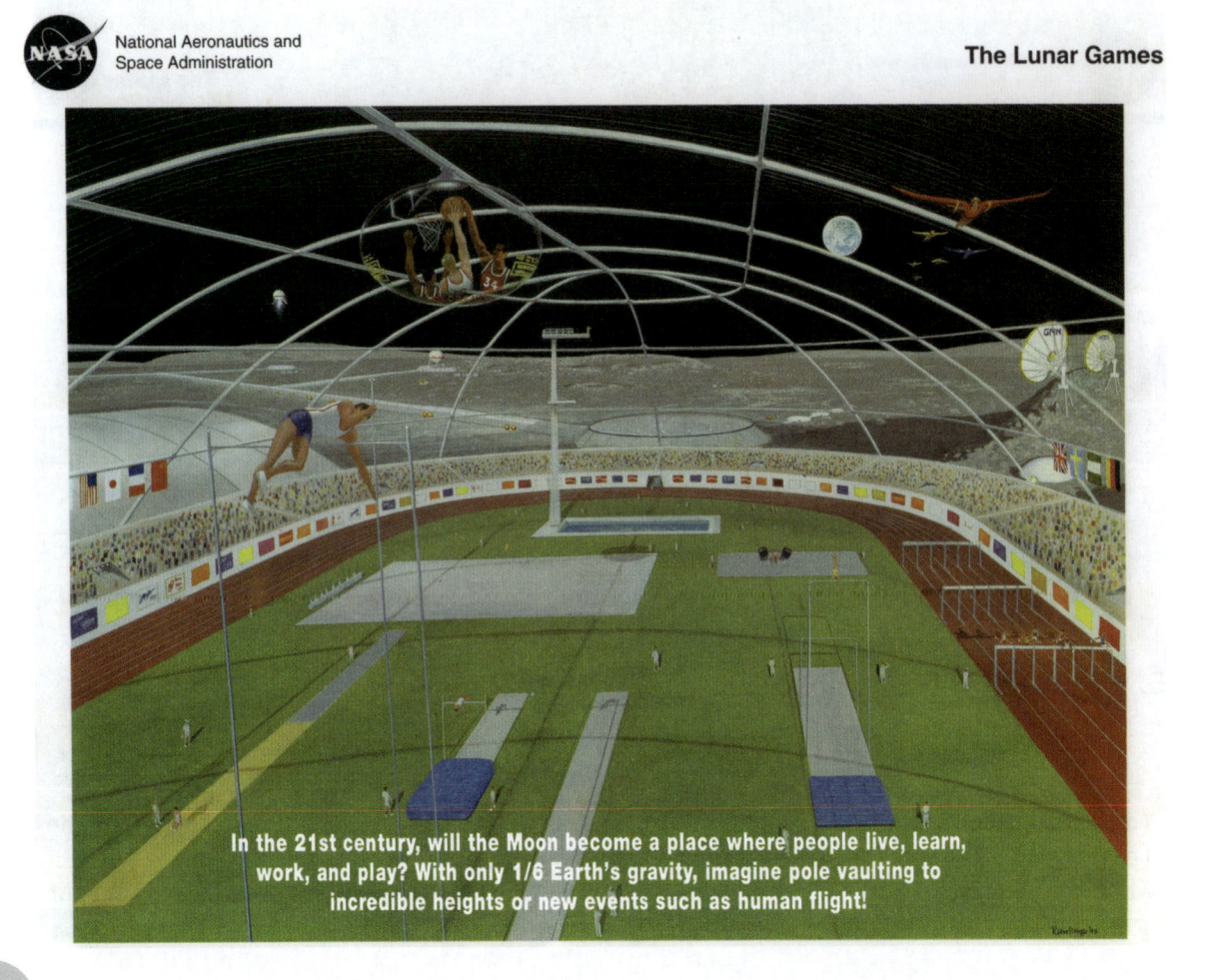

NASA National Aeronautics and Space Administration

The Lunar Games

In the 21st century, will the Moon become a place where people live, learn, work, and play? With only 1/6 Earth's gravity, imagine pole vaulting to incredible heights or new events such as human flight!

2. What is the brochure about? How do you know?

3. What kind of information did you find?

4. Now read and translate the paragraph in the picture.

5. Read this quotation about the future. Do you agree with it?

"In the end, our society will be defined not only by what we create but by what we refuse to destroy."

John Sawhill, former President of the Nature Conservancy.
Available at: <www.stthomas.edu/recycle/future.htm>. Accessed on: Nov. 15th, 2011.

6. Discuss with your classmates.

   a) How often do you think about your life and your community's life in the future?

   b) Should we worry about the future? Why? Why not?

   c) How will mankind be able to explore space in the future?

Don't miss!

LABBÉ, Brigite; PUECH, Michel. **Liberdade e responsabilidade**. São Paulo: Scipione, 2008.
Livro que apresenta questionamentos sobre valores humanos básicos como liberdade e responsabilidade.

🎧 Listen ➡️

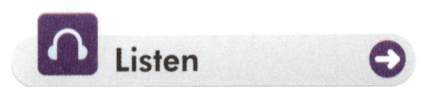

1. Look at the picture. What's going on?

   I think I'll buy some new shoes.

2. Now listen to the sentences. Match the sentences you hear to the pictures. 🎵 TRACK 10

3. Take a break and have fun with Garfield.

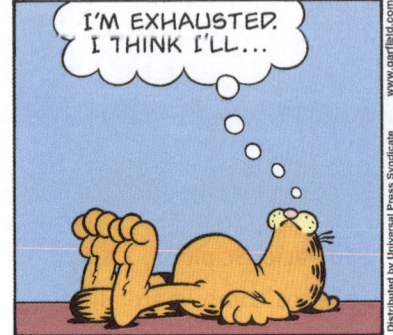

   I'M EXHAUSTED. I THINK I'LL...

   KEEP DOING THIS

   Available at: <www.garfield.com>. Accessed on: Nov. 15th, 2011.

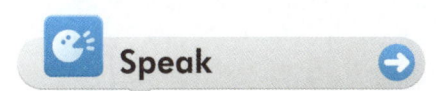

Speak

1. Complete the survey with the verbs from the box. Then check (✓) if you agree or disagree with the statements.

   be – waste – ~~know~~ – live – rain – have – smoke

   # ARE YOU AN OPTIMIST?

   By the year 2050,...

   a) We will **know** how to grow food in the ocean.
   ( ) Agree   ( ) Disagree

   b) We won't _____ any more wars.
   ( ) Agree   ( ) Disagree

   c) People will _____ and play different kinds of sports on the Moon.
   ( ) Agree   ( ) Disagree

   d) It will _____ hotter.
   ( ) Agree   ( ) Disagree

   e) It won't _____ enough.
   ( ) Agree   ( ) Disagree

   f) People won't _____ water.
   ( ) Agree   ( ) Disagree

   g) People will _____ less.
   ( ) Agree   ( ) Disagree

Don't miss!

França é o país mais deprimido do mundo. **Super Interessante**, São Paulo, 9 de dezembro de 2011. Edição 299.

Estudo foi feito em 18 países e mostra que nas nações ricas as pessoas têm mais depressão do que nas pobres – mas o Brasil aparece em terceiro no *ranking*.

Fonte: Cross-National Epidemiology of DSM.

Grammar points

By the year 2050, robots <u>will cook</u> our meals.

We use <u>WILL</u> + VERB (infinitive form) to talk about things that will take place in the future.

Remember that:

- Use the infinitive form of the verb after **will** or **won't**.
  More people will be vegetarians.
  There won't be any more pollution.
- Use contractions of **will** with all the subject pronouns in speaking and informal writing.

AFFIRMATIVE FORM	NEGATIVE FORM	INTERROGATIVE FORM
I You He 'll She will leave tomorrow. It We You They	I You He will not She won't leave tomorrow. It We You They	I you he Will she leave tomorrow? it we you they

- Do not use contractions in affirmative short answers.
  A: Will you be here?   B: Yes, I will.
- We use **will**:
  a) To make predictions: In 2050 cars will use solar energy.
  b) To make promise: She'll be back in ten minutes.
  c) To offer something: Don't worry. I'll help you.
- **Won't** is the contraction of **will + not**.
  The world will not be too crowded. = The world won't be too crowded.
- We use <u>probably</u> to say that something is not definite:
  People will probably take memory pills.
- Adverbs of time used with **will**:
  – Today, tonight, tomorrow
  – This morning, this afternoon, this evening
  – Tomorrow, tomorrow morning / tomorrow afternoon / tomorrow evening / tomorrow night
  – Next week/next month/next year/next Sunday/next summer/next weekend
  – In 2050, in the 23rd century, in ten years, in five weeks, in seven days

Vocabulary

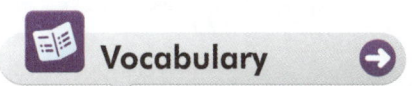

1. Look, listen and repeat.

Turn on

Turn off

Call up

Throw away

Put on

Take off

Make up

Hand in

Put away

2. What will Cate do tomorrow?

a) She will turn on the TV.

b) _____.

c) _____.

d) _____.

e) _____.

f) _____.

g) _____.

h) _____.

i) _____.

Remember that:

Turn on / Turn off
the TV
the radio
the lights
the computer
the CD player
the cellphone

Put on / Take off
your coat
your shoes
your sneakers
your watch
your cap

Call up
your parents
your friend(s)

Hand in
your homework
your composition

43

Write

1. Amaze your friends by looking into the future and reading fortunes with this awesome device.

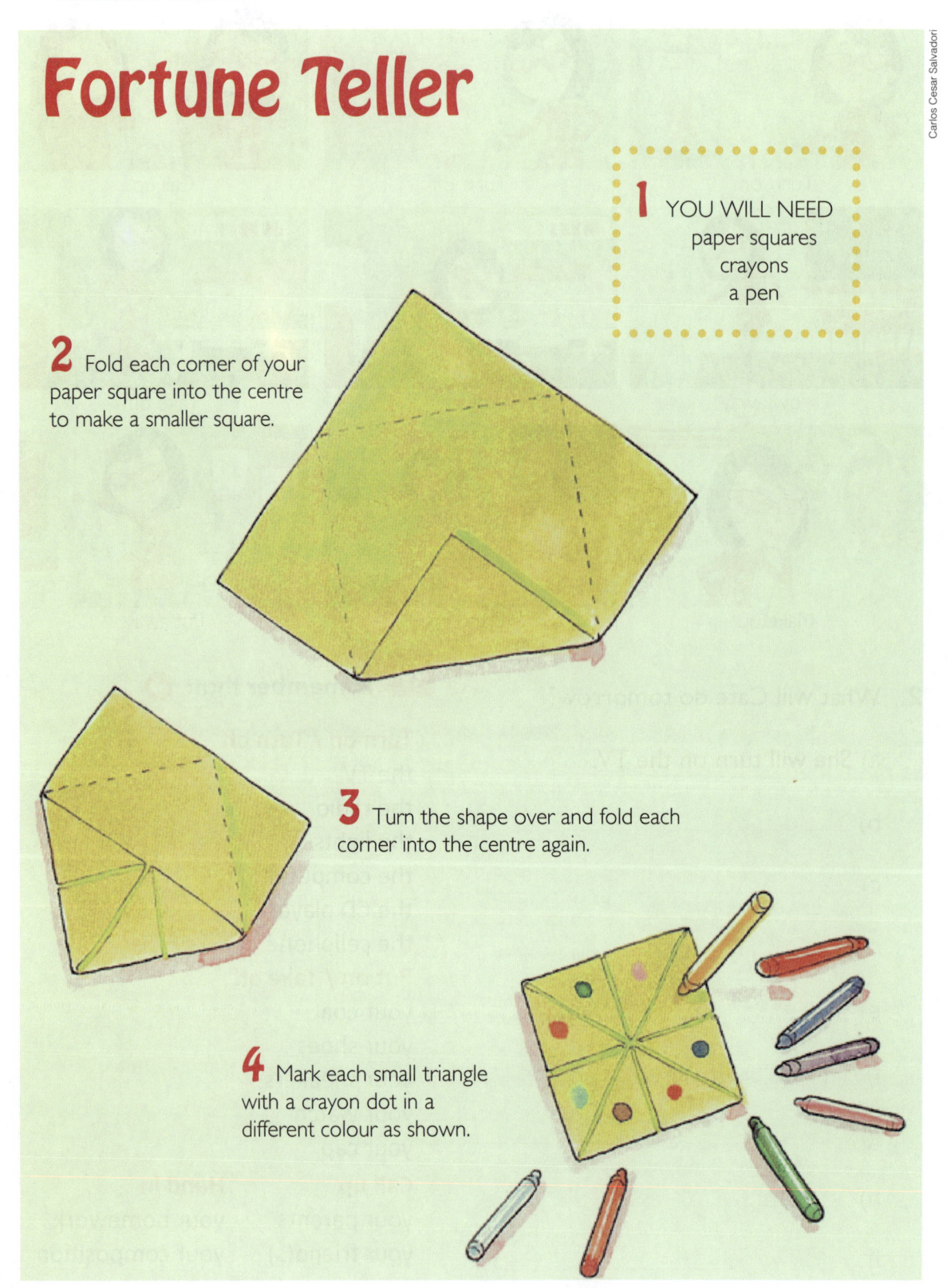

Fortune Teller

1 YOU WILL NEED
paper squares
crayons
a pen

2 Fold each corner of your paper square into the centre to make a smaller square.

3 Turn the shape over and fold each corner into the centre again.

4 Mark each small triangle with a crayon dot in a different colour as shown.

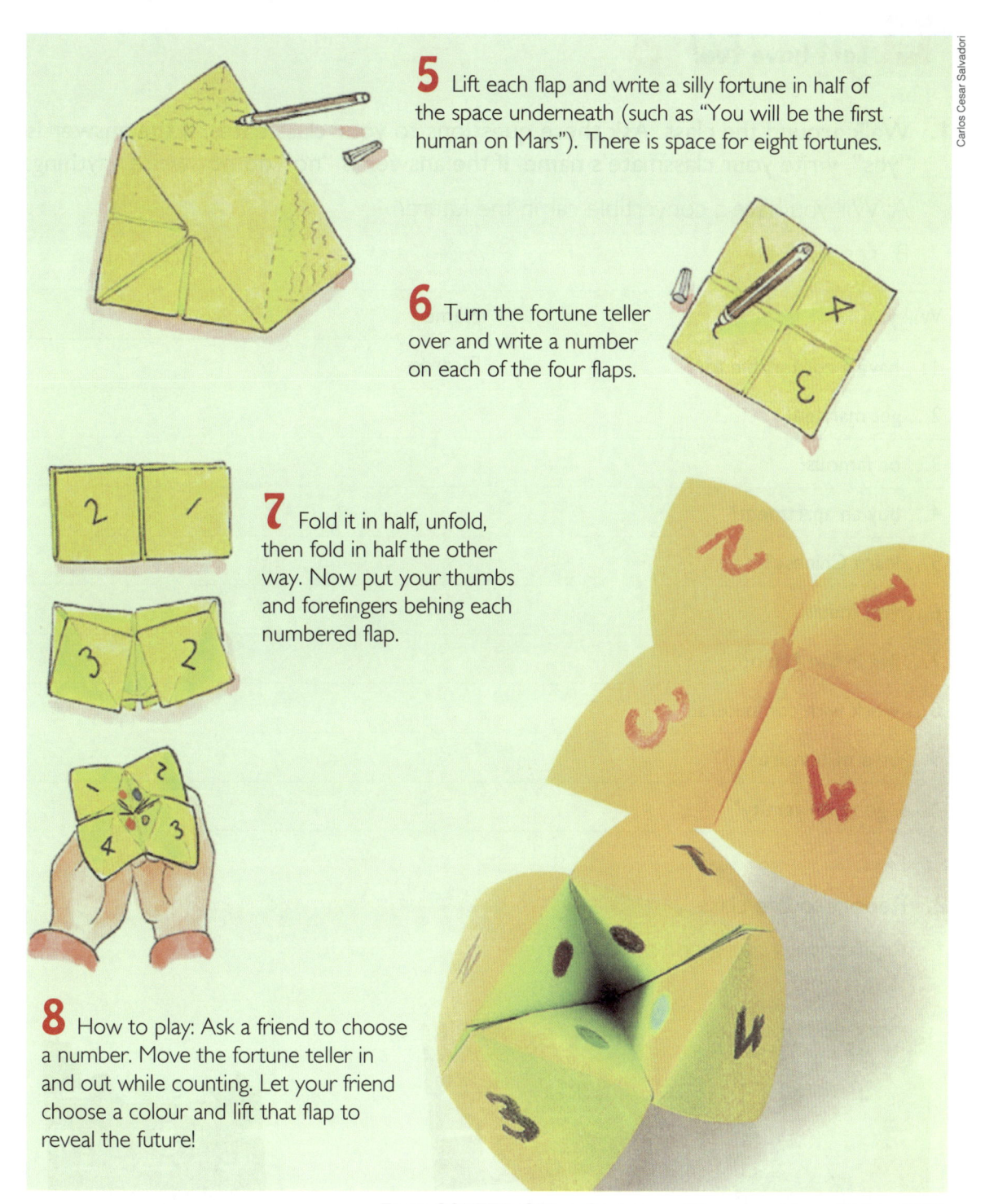

5 Lift each flap and write a silly fortune in half of the space underneath (such as "You will be the first human on Mars"). There is space for eight fortunes.

6 Turn the fortune teller over and write a number on each of the four flaps.

7 Fold it in half, unfold, then fold in half the other way. Now put your thumbs and forefingers behing each numbered flap.

8 How to play: Ask a friend to choose a number. Move the fortune teller in and out while counting. Let your friend choose a colour and lift that flap to reveal the future!

From: SOUTER, Gillian. **Games and Toys**. Lewisham: Kidbiz, 2000.

2. First write eight fortunes here. Then copy them to the fortune teller.

Ex.: You will get an "A" in a test.

_____

_____

_____

45

🌟 **Let's have fun!** ➡️

1. Walk around the class. Ask these questions to your classmates. If the answer is "yes", write your classmate's name. If the answer is "no" do not write anything.

   A: Will you have a convertible car in the future?
   B: Yes, I will.

Will you…	Name
1… have a convertible car?	Ricardo
2… get married?	
3… be famous?	
4… buy an apartment?	
5… learn Chinese?	
6… visit India?	
7… live in São Paulo?	
8… work with computers?	
9… be a millionaire?	
10… go to university?	

2. Report to the class.

   Ricardo will have a convertible car.

Exercise the mind

Warm-up: What are your predictions for your future?

Are you optimistic about the future?

Do you believe you will find a job doing the things you enjoy?

Do you think you will travel and have a home and a family?

TIME LINE ABOUT THE FUTURE

Teenagers are confident that social changes and new forms of technology will make their lives much better as they get older. Some teenagers say that "this is a great moment to grow up".

What about you? How do you feel about the future?

Look at Marina Bianchini. She's a fourteen-year-old Brazilian student from Curitiba, Paraná. Look at her time line:

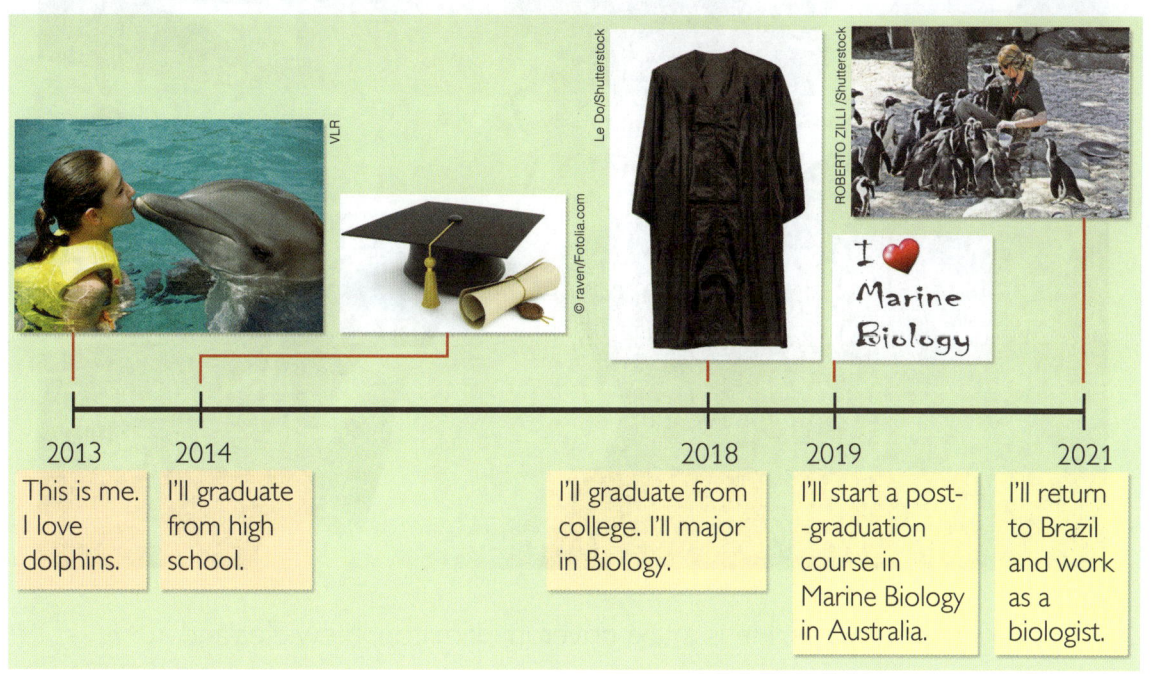

2013 — This is me. I love dolphins.

2014 — I'll graduate from high school.

2018 — I'll graduate from college. I'll major in Biology.

2019 — I'll start a post-graduation course in Marine Biology in Australia.

2021 — I'll return to Brazil and work as a biologist.

Now it's your turn.

- Make a time line of your future. Write the things you think will happen in your future. Be positive! Find or draw pictures of the events.
- Show your time line. Talk to your classmates about the future.

A: I'll travel around Brazil.

B: I'll study in England. What about you?

Review 2: UNIT 3/4

1. Write the sentences. Use <u>can</u>, <u>can't</u>, <u>could</u> or <u>couldn't</u>.

    a) When my grandmother was fifteen, she **could** visit her friends on the weekends.

    b) Sarah _____ use a cellphone during school breaks.

    c) The students _____ study in the library last year. This year they can.

    d) _____ you close the window, please? It's cold inside the classroom.

    e) When my dad was five years old he _____ ride his bike in the playground. He was very smart.

2. Read the text about the taxi driver. Underline the correct alternatives.

This is Gregory Hymes. He is a taxi driver in Hamilton, New Zealand.

I can / <u>could</u> drive my father's car when I was eighteen. It was easier in the past because there wasn't too much traffic. Today you has to / have to drive very carefully and you have to / don't have to be careful not to get lost. If you want you can / must talk to the passengers but you must / might pay attention while you drive. You shouldn't / couldn't argue with them. The pay isn't very good, so I must / mustn't work hard everyday. I can / should choose to work on the weekends, but happily I have to / don't have to work on Sundays.

3. Look at the verbs below. Add the corresponding endings (-able, -ible, -ary / -ory, -ant/ent, or –ful) and write the adjectives in the corresponding columns.

> accept – waste – convert – persist – respect –
> please – regret – divide – revolutionise – regulate

-able

acceptable

_____

- ible

_____

_____

-ary / -ory

_____

-ant / ent

_____

_____

-ful

_____

_____

4. Look at the picture of Ricardo as he imagines his life in twenty years. Write sentences about him.

a) **He will be an engineer**.

b) _____.

c) _____.

d) _____.

e) _____.

f) _____.

g) _____.

h) _____.

i) _____.

UNIT 5

AFRICA

- Past Progressive Form – Biography – Talking about Africa

WARM-UP: What is a tree good for?

How do trees benefit humans or animals?

Make a list and exchange ideas with your classmates.

Read

1. Look at this tree. Read the text quickly. What words do you know?

The African Baobab is also called the Monkey Bread Tree because baboons love eating its fruit, and the **Bottle Tree** because of its enormous swollen trunk. 2000-year-old baobabs can have fantastic girths of 10 meters in diameter!

Baobab leaves are not just eaten by cattle, browsing elephants and impala. They are rich in vitamin C and can be cooked like spinach or dried and made into soups and sauces. The leaves are also used as medicine to treat fevers, insect bites and diarrhea.

Baobab flowers are large, white and waxy, with big yellow stamens. They begin to open around sunset but only last until the next morning. They give off a strong rotting smell which attracts bats, bluebottles and nocturnal moths.

Baobab fruits are woody hanging pods, covered in velvety yellow-brown hair. The seeds in ripe fruit are held in place by delicious sweet white pulp that tastes just like wine gums! When the heavy fruits fall from the tree, the woody casing cracks open and termites eat the fruit, leaving the seeds to be carried away by monkeys, baboons, squirrels and rats.

The hollowed-out trunks of baobabs are often used for storing water. A large tree can hold up to 2000 gallons. Hollowed-out baobabs have been used for many weird and wonderful things. They have been prisons, stables, bus shelters, dairies and a weaver's workshop. One baobab tree even had a flush toilet installed in it!

The baobab is home to many other insects and birds in addition to those mentioned in the **book**. King Baboon spiders, bees, mealy bugs, caterpillars and stick insects all live in the tree. Parrots, hornbills and kingfishers roost or nest in holes in the trunk, while lovebirds, barn owls and Wahlberg's eagles nest in the branches. And, dangling out on the ends of the highest branches, far away from predators, are the little buffalo-weaver birds' round basket nests.

Baobab roots can be cooked and eaten or made into red dye. They are also made into a dried powder to take as a medicine for malaria or as a mouthwash for a toothache.

The strange shape of the baobab has inspired many stories. One says that the first baobab always complained wherever God planted it. In the end God became so fed up that he threw the tree away into the dry soil of the African plain -- where it landed upside down! Some say that spirits live in the flowers, so that if you pick a flower, you will be killed by a lion. In Nigeria, religious symbols have been found cut into the bark of ancient trees, suggesting that the trees were worshipped as fertility symbols in the past.

Baobab bark is extraordinary, because when it is cut or damaged it heals itself, just like our skin. Root bark is used to make strings for musical instruments or rope for making fishing nets. In parts of Africa, the fibers are woven into waterproof hats that are also used as drinking cups.

Baobab wood is very spongy as it is full of stored water. It is used to make **plates**, trays and floats for fishing.

From: MOSS, Miriam; KENNAWAY, Adrienne. This is the tree: A Story of the Baobab. Tulsa: EDC Publishing, 2005.

2. The Baobab tree is a characteristic tree in the African savannah landscape. It is used in many ways by animals and humans. Research the internet to find out more about this tree.

51

Listen

1. True or False? Listen and check.

a) (　) True　　　b) (　) True　　　c) (　) True
　 (　) False　　　 (　) False　　　 (　) False

d) (　) True　　　e) (　) True　　　f) (　) True
　 (　) False　　　 (　) False　　　 (　) False

2. Listen again and answer the questions.

a) What time did the bell ring?
   It rang at 8:30 a.m.

b) Where were the students?
   _____

c) Were Mrs. Costa and Mr. Rufino in the classroom?
   _____

d) Who is the geography teacher?
   _____

e) What were the students doing at 8:45 when she walked into the classroom according to the CD?
   _____
   _____
   _____

f) What was Lyndon doing?
   _____

Speak

What about you? Talk about the questions with your classmates.

> What were you doing when the teacher walked into the classroom today?

_____
_____

> What was your teacher doing when you walked into the classroom today?

_____
_____

Grammar points

1. Look at the sentences below:

When the bell <u>rang</u> the students <u>were waiting</u> for Mrs. Weber.

SIMPLE PAST (shorter action) PAST PROGRESSIVE (longer action)

Remember that:

- We use the Simple Past to talk about events or actions that finished at a specific time in the past.
- We use the Past Progressive to talk about events or actions that were in progress at a specific time in the past.
- Look at how we form the Past Progressive in the:
  – Affirmative form
  Laura was listening to the music.
  SUBJECT + WAS / WERE + V (ING) + COMPLEMENT

  – Negative form
  Gabriela and Sarah weren't laughing in the classroom.
  SUBJECT + WASN'T / WEREN'T + V (ING) + COMPLEMENT

  – Interrogative form
  Were Cate and Ricardo writing on the board?
  WAS / WERE + SUBJECT + V (ING) + COMPLEMENT

2. Work with a classmate. Read the events below. Then write the verbs in the corresponding forms.

I **went** to bed at 10:00 last night.
(go)

I _____ when it _____ to rain heavily.
(sleep)   (start)

When I _____ early in the morning my dog _____.
(wake up)   (bark)

When I _____ he _____ his tail. He wanted to go out.
(get up)   (shake)

That's why I _____ a nap at school today.
(take)

Vocabulary

1. What were they doing at 7:30 p.m. yesterday evening? Complete the sentences with the Past Progressive. Listen and check.

a) At 7:30, my brother and I **were watching** (watch) a volleyball game in the school gym. Our school team _____ (play) really well and we _____ (win). Suddenly the lights went out and the game finished. We felt disappointed!

b) At 7:30, my family and I _____ (go) home. When we arrived we waited for the elevator. We _____ (ride) the elevator up to our apartment. Then the lights went out and the elevator stopped. We felt scared because we _____! (move)

c) At 7:30, I _____ (take) a shower at home. The water was warm and I _____ (sing) my favorite song. From one moment to another, it was dark. The lights went out and I felt cold!

d) At 7:30, I _____ (study) at home. There was a geography test early the next morning. I _____ (read) about the Baobab tree and all the magic of the African plain. Suddenly the lights went out and I felt desperate!

Remember that:

Other collocations with feel:

feel like: When I came back to Brazil, I felt like a stranger.

feel the need: He felt the need to talk to someone.

feel pain: She felt a sudden pain in her stomach.

Write

WARM-UP: Have you ever met any foreign people?
Have you ever met people from Africa?
Do you know any famous people from South Africa?

1. Look at the text below. What kind of text is it?

1. Say the name of the person in the first sentence.

Use the Simple Past to describe completed actions.

Use connectors to join ideas or give some more information. The most common are: after, and, also, besides, too, in addition, moreover, furthermore, as well, not only… but also, thereafter.

Other connectors are used to give extra information. The most common are: for example, for instance, like, such as, especially, particularly, in particular.

Nelson Rolihlahla Mandela was born in Transkei, South Africa on July 18, 1918. His father was Chief Henry Mandela of the Tembu Tribe. Mandela himself was educated at University College of Fort Hare and the University of Witwatersrand and qualified in law in 1942. He joined the African National Congress in 1944 and was engaged in resistance against the ruling National Party's apartheid policies after 1948. He went on trial for treason in 1956-1961 and was acquitted in 1961.

After the banning of the ANC in 1960, Nelson Mandela argued for the setting up of a military wing within the ANC. In June 1961, the ANC executive considered his proposal on the use of violent tactics and agreed that those members who wished to involve themselves in Mandela's campaign would not be stopped from doing so by the ANC. This led to the formation of Umkhonto we Sizwe. Mandela was arrested in 1962 and sentenced to five years' imprisonment with hard labour. In 1963, when many fellow leaders of the ANC and the Umkhonto we Sizwe were arrested, Mandela was brought to stand trial with them for plotting to overthrow the government by violence. His statement from the dock received considerable international publicity. On June 12, 1964, eight of the accused, including Mandela, were sentenced to life imprisonment. From 1964 to 1982, he was incarcerated at Robben Island Prison, off Cape Town; thereafter, he was at Pollsmoor Prison, nearby on the mainland.

During his years in prison, Nelson Mandela's reputation grew steadily. He was widely accepted as the most significant black leader in South Africa and became a potent symbol of resistance as the anti-apartheid movement gathered strength. He consistently refused to compromise his political position to obtain his freedom.

Nelson Mandela was released on February 11, 1990. After his release, he plunged himself wholeheartedly into his life's work, striving to attain the goals he and others had set out almost four decades earlier. In 1991, at the first national conference of the ANC held inside South Africa after the organization had been banned in 1960, Mandela was elected President of the ANC while his lifelong friend and colleague, Oliver Tambo, became the organisation's National Chairperson.

From: Les Prix Nobel. The Nobel Prizes 1993, Editor Tore Frängsmyr, [Nobel Foundation] © Nobel Foundation 1993. Stockholm, 1994. <http://www.nobelprize.org/nobel_prizes/peace/laureatis/1993/mandela-lecture.html>. Accessed on: November 28, 2011.

2. Say when he was born and where he is from.

3. Give a short description to attract the reader's attention.

4. Describe the accomplishments of the person.

5. End your biography by saying why you admire this person.

2. Mandela's work has been recognized worldwide. He has become not only South Africa's most famous and admired leader but he has also received many honorary degrees from universities all over the world. Do you know which prize he received in 1993?

_____

3. Now it's your turn. Here are some steps to write a biography.

a) Choose the person you are going to write about. Who is he /she?

_____

b) Write a short biography. Use the Simple Past tense or the Past Progressive. Include the person's name in the first sentence.

_____

c) Then say when the person is / was born and where the person is / was from.

_____

d) Write about this person's accomplishment.

e) Say why this person is important and in which area (medicine, arts, history, etc.)

f) Remember to end your biography telling the reader why you admire this person.

g) Write the biography here. If you prefer, you can write it in your notebook.

_____
_____
_____
_____
_____
_____
_____
_____
_____
_____

AFRICA
South Africa

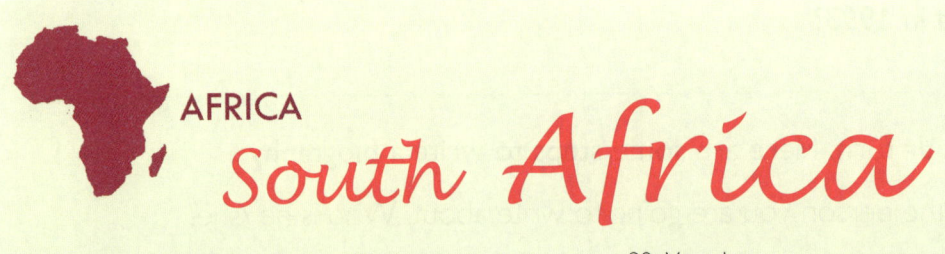

CROSSWORD PUZZLE

ACROSS →

4. Wild animals in __ National Park are tourist attractions.
7. A policy of racial segregation is called __.
8. A poultry product.
9. A farm crop.
11. Chief farm-product export.
12. A leading fruit crop.
13. South Africa: most highly developed and __ country in Africa.
18. Many non-whites have low-__ jobs.
23. South of the equator: seasons are __ from the Northern Hemisphere.
15. A world leader in raising __.
16. Blacks are mostly __, miners, and laborers.
17. A wild animal in the National Park.
19. __ people control the government, but there are few of them.
20. Very dry area: __ Desert.
21. Many Asians (mostly Indians) sell vegetables or __ in factories.
22. Farmers produce nearly all the needed __.

Sheep

DOWN ↓

1. Most of the people are __ Africans.
2. Most whites, whose ancestors were usually from the Netherlands, Germany, or France, are called __.
3. South Africa: approximately __ times as large as California.
5. Johannesburg area: world's richest __ field.
6. The government divides South Africa into four __ groups: Whites, Coloreds, Asians, Blacks.
9. Three capitals: __ Town, Pretoria, and Bloemfontein.
10. South Africa's longest river: __ River.
14. Whites from __, Scotland, and Ireland are business people.

4 ACROSS: KRUGER
7 ACROSS: APARTHEID

From CHEYNEY, Jeanne and Arnold. The Continents: Puzzles for Learning World Geography. Glenview: GoodYearBooks, 1994.

Exercise the mind

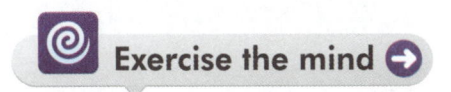

WARM UP: Do you celebrate Christmas?

If you don't, do you celebrate a different holiday?

What do you know about similar holidays in other cultures?

KWANZAA

Kwanzaa is a seven-day African American holiday which starts on December 26 and lasts until the first of January. It has no ties with any religion or political issues. It celebrates African American people, their lives, their history and their culture.

A great feast called the Kamaru is held on the night of December 31st and houses are decorated in the traditional colors of black unity: red, black and green.

Kinara is the candle holder used in Kwanzaa celebrations.

Each family has a candle holder called a kinara. It holds 7 candles and one candle is lit each day during Kwanzaa. The three candles on the right are green and represent hope, and the land of Africa. One black candle in the center represents the unity and race of African people. The candles on the left stands for African blood shed.

Many people mistake it for an African American form of Christmas because it occurs the day after Christmas.

Exchanging ideas

- What kind of celebration is it?

_____

- When is Kwanzaa celebrated?

_____

- Do people celebrate Kwanzaa in Brazil?

Click

<http://pessoas.hsw.uol.com.br/kwanzaa.htm>. Acesso em: 28 nov. 2011.
Site que fala sobre a história, princípios e tradições dessa celebração.

UNIT 6

HAVE YOU EVER BEEN TO NEW ZEALAND?

- Present Perfect – Talking about experiences – Using commas – Talking about New Zealand

WARM-UP: Have you ever been to New Zealand?
Do you know where New Zealand is?
Would you like to visit New Zealand?

Read

1. Read the text quickly. Answer the questions, but don't look at the text carefully.

   a) Juliana Varela was _____ in New Zealand.

   b) She worked with _____ in New Zealand.

   c) She's from _____.

2. What type of text is it?

3. This is Juliana Varela. She lived in Auckland, New Zealand from 2008 to 2011. She used to work as a General Manager for Discovery Education & Travel. She was in charge of taking care of the exchange students that decided to spend six months or one year as high school students. In this interview, Mrs. Varela talks about some hints about living and studying in New Zealand. Listen to her interview.

Where are you originally from?
I am from Curitiba, Brazil.

How long did you live in New Zealand?
I spent 3 years in New Zealand.

Was it easy meeting people and making friends when you arrived there?
People in New Zealand(NZ) are nice and friendly so it was easy to make new friends. They love happy hour after work and "barbies" during the weekend. (Barbie is the way the Kiwis call Barbecue).

People from New Zealand, descendants of English and Irish people.

What was your job at Discovery Education & Travel?

I used to work as a General Manager and my main duties were:
– Financial and human resources; – Counselor to students during the exchange program in NZ; – Relationship with partner schools; – Responsible for planning and execution of trips to New Zealand and Australia; – Responsible for marketing strategies.

Where did most students come from?

Most of the students were from Brazil, Germany and Spain, but there were always some students from Italy and Mexico as well.

Were there many students coming from Brazil?

There are a lot of students from Brazil in NZ. Brazilians and Kiwis get along very well so I believe that is the reason they choose to go to NZ.

Where did they stay?

There are students all over the country, from Kerikeri (north of North Island) to Dunedin (very south of the South Island). And they always live in homestays, families prepared to receive students from abroad.

What was their common daily routine at schools?

In New Zealand, school starts at 8:30 and finishes at 3:30. After that they usually practice some sport and go home around 6:30. Dinner in NZ is the main meal and it is around 7 p.m. After that they have some time with the family and they go to bed around 10 p.m., much earlier than the Brazilians.

What were the students' most frequent complaints?

Usually complaints happened in the beginning of the program when the students are homesick, missing family and friends and when they have to accept the new way of living in a different country and a new language. After one or two months when the students are feeling at home, the problem is when they have to go home, because they really love the program and always want to stay longer.

Tell me three words that best describe your experience in New Zealand.

Exciting. Unforgettable. Extreme.

4. Listen and read the text again. What is the interview about?

5. Now find the information below in the text.

   a) Juliana's hometown: **Curitiba**

   b) Nationalities of students going to New Zealand:
   _____
   _____

   c) Cities where exchange students stay in New Zealand:
   _____

   d) School time in New Zealand:
   _____

This is a souvenir from New Zealand. You can see the Kiwi, the national symbol of New Zealand, a bird that doesn't fly and has its nocturnal habits.

Listen

1. Listen to Gabriela and David. Look at the pictures. Then match the corresponding paragraphs to the pictures.

a)

David: Who are you going with?

Gabriela: I'm going with a group of Brazilian students.

David: How do you feel?

Gabriela: I feel excited!

b)

a

Gabriela: David, look!

David: What is it, Gabriela?

Gabriela: It's an airplane ticket. I'm going to New Zealand on a student exchange program.

David: That's cool! When are you going?

Gabriela: Next year. I'll be there for one term.

c)

David: I'm glad you're going to New Zealand.

Gabriela: Me too. It will be a wonderful experience.

d)

David: Have you ever been to New Zealand?

Gabriela: No, I haven't. I've never been out of Brazil.

Speak

1. Look, listen and repeat. TRACK 16

EATEN SUSHI

SEEN A PENGUIN

BEEN TO SÃO PAULO

BAKED COOKIES

GONE FISHING

FLOWN IN A BALLOON

SLEPT IN A TENT

CHEATED ON A TEST

2. Talk to a classmate about your experience. Use the dialogue below as a model.

Have you ever eaten sushi?

Yes, I have.

And you?

No, I haven't.

3. Now write your answers for the questions below:

a) Have you ever eaten sushi?

_____

b) Have you ever seen a penguin?

_____

c) Have you ever been to São Paulo?

_____

d. Have you ever flown in a balloon?

_____

e) Have you ever slept in a tent?

_____

Grammar points

Gabriela is on her way to New Zealand. She has been on an airplane before, but she has never been out of the country. She can't wait to visit the beautiful city of Auckland. She has never been to New Zealand and she has never used the New Zealand dollar. She has never spoken to a Neozealander person, and she has never eaten their typical dishes. Gabriela is going to try all these things for the first time.

1. Look at the chart below. Listen and repeat the corresponding forms of the verbs.

INFINITIVE	PAST FORM	PAST PARTICIPLE	INFINITIVE	PAST FORM	PAST PARTICIPLE
eat	ate	eaten	sleep	slept	slept
see	saw	seen	cheat	cheated	cheated
be	was, were	been	have	had	had
bake	baked	baked	use	used	used
go	went	gone	speak	spoke	spoken
fly	flew	flown	write	wrote	written

Remember that:

- We use the Present Perfect to talk about things that happened at some time in the past.
- We can use <u>ever</u> with the Present Perfect in questions (ever = at any time in your life)
Have you ever met a famous pop star?
Has your mother ever danced tango?
- We can use <u>never</u> with the Present Perfect in negative answers.
(never = at no time in your life)
I have never studied German.
They have never seen a lion.
- Look at how to use the Present Perfect:
We use has / have + past participle (verb) or hasn't / haven't + past participle (verb)

AFFIRMATIVE	NEGATIVE	INTERROGATIVE
I have been to France. = I've been to France. She has seen Brazilian movies. = She's seen Brazilian movies.	I have not been to France. = I haven't been to France. She has not seen Brazilian movies. = She hasn't seen Brazilian movies.	Have you ever been to France? Yes, I have. No, I haven't. Has she ever seen Brazilian movies? Yes, she has. No, she hasn't.

Vocabulary

EXPERIENCES

1. Ask a classmate questions about his / her experiences. Put a check mark (✓) if your classmate has done it or an (X) if not.

A: Have you ever played golf?
B: Yes, I have. (✓) / No, I haven't. (X)

a)

Play golf

b)

Break a window

c)

Listen to a rock concert

d)

Have a pet fish

e)

See a UFO

f)

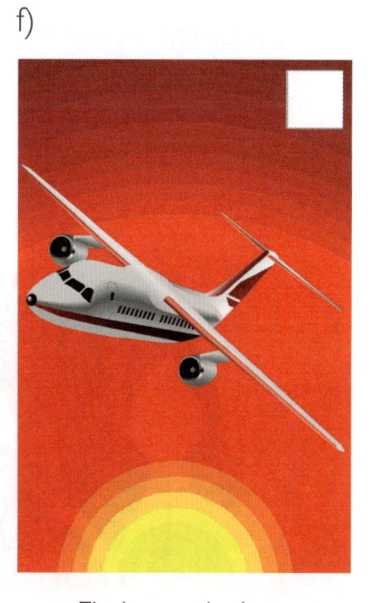

Fly in an airplane

65

Write

1. Do you know how to use commas (**,**) in English?

COMMAS MAKE THINGS CLEARER

Writers use punctuation marks to help make their writing clear. One very helpful punctuation mark is the comma (**,**) because it separates parts of a sentence. Let's check some rules that will teach you where to place commas in order to make your sentences clear and effective.

a) Use commas and coordinating conjunctions (and, but, or, nor, for, yet) to join two simple sentences:

We could go to the park**,** or we could go to the movies.

My mother brought some chocolate**,** and I gladly accepted it.

b) Use a single comma to separate three or more items in a series:

I like pasta**,** sea food**,** and chicken.

Men have traveled across oceans**,** around the world**,** and to the moon.

c) Use a single comma to separate two or more adjectives preceding a noun:

The old**,** ugly house was still in use.

d) Use a pair of commas to indicate a nonessential element in the sentences:

Mrs. Costa**,** our teacher**,** is very demanding (the words <u>our teacher</u> are nonessential to the meaning of the sentences. They could be removed and the meaning would be unchanged: Mrs. Costa is very demanding).

e) Use a pair of commas to set off parenthetical words or expressions:

Lyndon**,** of course**,** likes to run.

Laura**,** on the contrary**,** prefers to swim.

2. Now let's practice. Circle the coordinating conjunctions in each of the following sentences.

a) I would like to come, (but) I don't have time.

b) The sun has just set, yet there's still light outside.

c) He has not written, nor has called me.

d) They hit the ball, dropped the bat, and ran to the first base. It was a fantastic baseball game.

e) Gabriela can go to Florianópolis, or she can have a nice week in Porto Alegre.

3. Place commas where needed in the following sentences.

a) My meal consisted of soup**,** toast**,** and pasta.

b) Kazuki was reading David was writing and Sarah was doing the geography homework.

c) She has some orange juice a ham and cheese sandwich and eggs for breakfast.

d) The website is dedicated to Sarah Cate Gabriela and Laura.

e) Sarah's mother bought milk flour butter and eggs to make a cake.

4. Rewrite the following sentences, putting in commas where needed.

a) The person checking tickets at the counter asked for an identification card.
The person checking tickets, at the counter, asked for an identification card.

b) My grandmother who is seventy years old walks five blocks everyday.

c) The man who interviewed Mrs. Weber is the local newspaper reporter.

d) The movie that I wanted to see is no longer playing.

Let's have fun!

1. Do you remember Juliana Varela's interview on pages 60 and 61? She's back here to tell you a little bit more about New Zealand. Enjoy her points of view.

Interesting facts about New Zealand

By Juliana Varela

ENGLISH LANGUAGE

When we talk to New Zealanders, we can identify a difference in their accent, mainly if we are more familiar with American or British varieties. Among these differences, some examples are seven /ˈsevən/ that they pronounce /ˈsɪvən/ and left /left/ that they pronounce /lɪft/. Another difference is that they very often indicate the third person as SHE and not IT. Another interesting fact is the choice of words, many of which are spoken only in New Zealand, as TOGS = bikinis, HOODS = jacket with hood, BOOT = trunk, JANDALS = flip-flops, DAIRY = convenience store, BACH = summer house and the famous CHILLY BIN = a recipient to carry food and especially beer to the beach or the barbecue and keep it on ice.

HOLLYWOOD FILMS

New Zealand is a "Hollywood backyard" where a lot of movies and advertisements are recorded, because its natural beauty so easy to find everywhere. The movies are Lord of the Rings, The Last Samurai, King Kong, Narnia, Avatar, The Hobbit and others.

Avatar.

EXTREME SPORTS

If there is one place on earth where you can do all sorts of adventure, this place is New Zealand and more specific in the South of the South Island – Queenstown. In this place besides having the most beautiful landscape, you can find bungee jumps from 45 meters to 150 meters, skydive, paraglide or perhaps get a jetboat, a boat at full speed that goes through canyons. You can walk around volcanoes and ski in the morning then travel a bit and surf in the afternoon.

Look at Juliana. Would you be as brave as she was?

Exercise the mind

WARM-UP: Have you ever heard about the Maoris?

What about the Maori cultures?

TA MOKO, a particular form of tattooing for men and women, as a sign of cultural identity.

MAORI CULTURE

The Maori are the indigenous people of New Zealand. They were the ones who first arrived in the islands and have preserved their culture. They have a political party which is very respected and important to the country. Maoris make up about 10 % of the population. According to Juliana Varela, like in other countries, the minorities have social problems, including abuse of drugs and alcohol, unemployment and violence.

Did you know that?

- The Maori people call New Zealand Aotearoa, the land of the long white cloud;
- Look at the strong influence of the Maori language in English:
- WHANAU = family, AOTEAROA = New Zealand, MAKE TOO = very good, HAKA = a Maori war song, TE REO = the Maori language and the famous KIA ORA = which means a hello, thank you and good bye.
- The word "maori" means normal and ordinary. In Maori legends, it distinguished ordinary mortal humans from gods and spirits.
- Greetings: the traditional Maori welcome is called a hongi. It's a greeting that involves pressing noses instead of kissing.

Exchanging ideas

- What about you?
- What are other facts you would like to know about this magical community and its country?

Review 3: UNIT 5/6

1. What were the students doing when Mrs. Weber walked into the classroom?

a)

Gabriela and Sarah were dancing.

b)

c)

d)

2. Match the collocations with their corresponding meanings.

a) The weather was freezing yesterday.

b) Sarah lost her wallet.

c) We watched a horror movie last night.

d) His grades at math were very bad. And he studied a lot for the test.

( ) She felt desperate.

( ) He felt disappointed.

(a) I felt cold all night long.

( ) We felt scared!

3. Match the pictures and the sentences.

a) b) c)

d) e) f)

They have flown in an airplane.		She has broken the window.	
I have never seen a UFO.	a	Have you ever had a pet fish?	
He has played golf.		Has she ever listened to a rock concert?	

4. Place commas where needed in the following sentences.

a) She can speak Portuguese**,** or she can speak English.

b) Mrs. Weber the geography teacher is in the classroom.

c) The new fantastic car was blue.

d) I like ice cream chocolate and banana pie.

e) Sarah was eating Cate was listening to music and Gabriela was studying.

f) My father who is fifty years old drives his car to work everyday.

UNIT 7

BRAZIL, THE COUNTRY OF THE PRESENT

- Present Perfect – Yet /Already – Since/For – Positivizers

Read

1. Read the text quickly. Where do you think they come from? Who is the probable reader of these texts? What are the texts about?

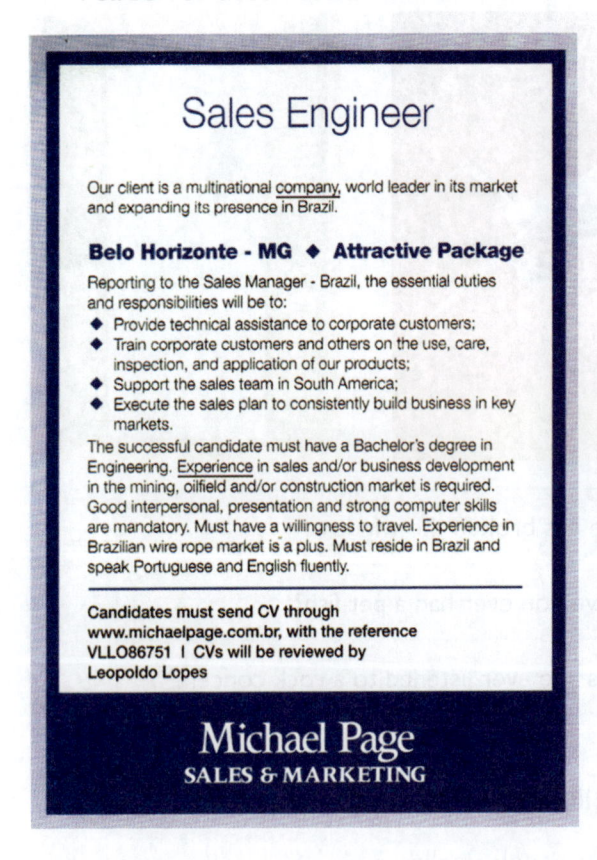

Sales Engineer

Our client is a multinational company, world leader in its market and expanding its presence in Brazil.

Belo Horizonte - MG ♦ Attractive Package

Reporting to the Sales Manager - Brazil, the essential duties and responsibilities will be to:
- Provide technical assistance to corporate customers;
- Train corporate customers and others on the use, care, inspection, and application of our products;
- Support the sales team in South America;
- Execute the sales plan to consistently build business in key markets.

The successful candidate must have a Bachelor's degree in Engineering. Experience in sales and/or business development in the mining, oilfield and/or construction market is required. Good interpersonal, presentation and strong computer skills are mandatory. Must have a willingness to travel. Experience in Brazilian wire rope market is a plus. Must reside in Brazil and speak Portuguese and English fluently.

Candidates must send CV through www.michaelpage.com.br, with the reference VLLO86751 | CVs will be reviewed by Leopoldo Lopes

Michael Page
SALES & MARKETING

Technical Sales Manager Animal Feed

Our client is a multinational chemical company with an annual revenue of 4 billion euros.

São Paulo - SP ♦ Salary + bonus + car

Reporting to the Area Business Manager, your main responsibilities will be:
- To sell company's products to the animal feed industry;
- Recruit and manage distributors and agents;
- Participate in industry associations, trade shows and conferences;
- Work with a global sales, marketing and technical team to develop new products and markets;
- Provide technical and marketing support to customers and business partners.

This manager must have a graduate degree in animal science, feed manufacturing or chemistry. The professional must have a solid technical sales experience in the feed industry or good experience in feed manufacturing with an aptitude for sales. Fluency in English is mandatory, desirable in Spanish.

Candidates must send CV through www.michaelpage.com.br, with the reference VFCU88848 | CVs will be reviewed by Fábio Cunha

Michael Page
SALES & MARKETING

From: Exame, Edição 989, Ano 45, n. 6. 6/4/2011. p. 134.

2. Match the words in the first column with their definitions in the second column. You may use a dictionary. Then look for the words on pages 72. Underline them.

WORDS

(   ) EXPERIENCE

(   ) COMPANY

(   ) LEADER

(   ) MANAGER

(   ) DUTIES

(a) RESPONSIBILITIES

(   ) FLUENCY

(   ) SALE(S)

(   ) CUSTOMER(S)

(   ) SALARY

(   ) TEAM

(   ) PARTNER

DEFINITIONS

a) Something for which one is responsible.

b) A group of people that carry on a commercial or industrial enterprise.

c) Fixed compensation paid regularly for services.

d) Someone who leads, manages and controls.

e) Obligatory tasks.

f) A member of a partnership especially in business.

g) Someone who purchases something from someone else.

h) Knowledge or skill or practice derived from direct observation.

i) The quality of being fluent.

j) A person who conducts business.

k) The act of selling.

l) A number of people associated together in work.

3. Read the quotation below. It's from Steve Jobs.

" You can't just ask customers what they want and then try to give that to them. By the time you get it built, they'll want something new."

From: <www.quotationspage.com/quotes/Steve-jobs>. Accessed on: Dec. 12th, 2011.

STEVE JOBS (1955 – 2011): Pioneer of the personal computer revolution.

4. Do you agree with Steve Jobs quotation? Why? / Why not?

73

Listen

1. Ricardo is talking to Gabriela. Look at the pictures below. What do you think they're talking about?

Ricardo: Hi, Gabriela. I knew your parents were having a new house built.

Gabriela: That's right. They have dreamed of having their own house built since they were just married.

Ricardo: What kind of house are they having built?

Gabriela: They chose a detached house.

Ricardo: What kind of house is it?

Gabriela: It's a house that stands alone. It doesn't share a common wall.

Ricardo: Oh, I see. When did your parents start having it built?

Gabriela: They have worked on the house for about one year. It's a slow process, but my aunt Lúcia, do you remember her? She's an architect and she has helped them on the weekends on the project.

Ricardo: So, have they reached the roof yet?

Gabriela: No, they haven't done the roof yet. But they have already done the floors, doors and windows. It's beginning to look like a real house now!

Ricardo: And, as I can see, you look excited about the new house, the project… By the way, would you like to be an architect like your aunt in the future?

Gabriela: You got it! It's a fantastic profession.

Ricardo: It is. But remember that you have to study hard and be prepared for the work market.

Gabriela: I know it. That's why I'm going to New Zealand. An international experience is a must in any curriculum vitae nowadays.

2. Check (✓) how Gabriela's house will look according to the dialogue. Then label them.

a)

b)

Speak

1. Underline <u>already</u> and <u>yet</u> in the dialogue, exercise 1 on page 74.

2. Complete the rules with <u>already</u> and <u>yet</u>.

   a) We use <u>already</u>:
   - In affirmative sentences:
     We have **already** had our lunch.
   - After <u>have</u> and <u>before</u> the past participle of the main verb:
     The students have _____ studied for the test.
   - When an action has happened sooner than expected:
     She has _____ finished her work.

   b) We use <u>yet</u>:
   - In negative sentences and questions.
     Has the letter arrived _____?
     No, it hasn't. It hasn't arrived _____.
   - At the end of the sentences.
     The bus hasn't come _____.
   - When we think that an action will happen soon:
     Gabriela hasn't visited New Zealand _____.

3. Make a list of three things you have done and four things you plan to do soon.

DONE	PLAN TO DO
MODEL: do homework	Go camping

4. In pairs, ask and answer questions about your list above. Use <u>already</u> or <u>yet</u>.

   A: Have you done your homework yet?

   B: Yes, I have. I have already done it.

Grammar points

1. Read the example sentences and complete the rules.

Remember that:

Use the Present Perfect with *for* and *since* to talk about something that began in the past and continues into the present (and may continue into the future):

They have dreamed of having their own house built *since* they were just married. They have worked on the house for about one year.

a) We use *for*:
- To refer to the duration of an action.
  How long has she lived in Curitiba?
  She has lived in Curitiba for a long time.
  Use *for* + length of time (for 15 minutes, for one week, for two years) to show how long something has lasted.

b) We use *since*:
- To refer to the moment when an action started:
  How long have you lived in Curitiba?
  I have lived in Curitiba since 2009.

- Use *since* + point of time (since yesterday, since 1:00, since Tuesday, since 1990) to show when something started.

2. Complete the table with the time expressions in the corresponding columns.

twenty minutes	last winter	one month
a day	I was a child	the 1980s
yesterday	October 24th	2011
two weeks	five o'clock	seven years

FOR	SINCE
twenty minutes	

Vocabulary

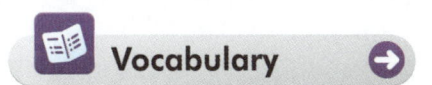

1. Look at the pictures. Write the questions. Use the clues to help you.

2. Choose the correct answers from the box and copy them into each picture.

> Yes, I have already put away my clothes.
> Yes, I have already finished on the phone.
> ~~No, I haven't cleaned it yet.~~
> No, I haven't done the washing up yet.

a) You / clean / your room / yet?

- Have you cleaned your room yet?
- No, I haven't cleaned it yet.

b) You / finish / on the phone / yet?

- Have you finished on the phone yet?

c) You / do / the washing up / yet?

- Have you done the washing up yet?

d) You / put away / your clothes / yet?

- Have you put away your clothes yet?

Write

WORKING WITH POSITIVE VERBS

1. Go back to page 72. What is it about?

2. Why are classified ads important to you?

3. What kind of world do you expect for you?

4. According to Matos (2004), "Language use is the most humanizing force". Do you agree with him?

5. Matos, who is a Brazilian professor from Crato, Ceará, has created what he calls "positivizers". They are words and expressions related to positive human qualities. He believes that we can use language to communicate for the good. Look at one list he has created with this objective. Use a dictionary to check the words you may not know. Listen to the sentences.

Advise and advocate rather than admonish.

Be a peaceful bridge between Brazilians.

Contribute to a culture of compassion.

Defend democracy with determination.

Express empathy and encouragement.

Foster freedom and friendship.

Generate goodness and generosity.

Honor humanism and humanitarianism.

Inspire interdependence and integration.

Join the family of justice joyfully.

Keep kindling your kindness to others.

Let love be your light.

Maximize mediation and meditation.

Nourish and nurture non-violence.

Opt for an original and optimistic vocabulary.

Prepare yourself as a peace patriot.

Respect and reassure, for reconciliation.

Support and sustain solidarity.

Teach in a spirit of tact and tolerance.

Upgrade universal feelings of unity.

Weigh your words wisely.

6. What does each sentences reveal? What kind of values do they translate? (civic, ethical, moral, social, etc…).

_____

7. Now it's your turn. You are going to create your list with "positivizers".

   a) First think about a list of positive adjectives (adjectives related to positive human qualities).
   There are examples for you. Complete the list. Use your dictionary. Talk to your classmates.

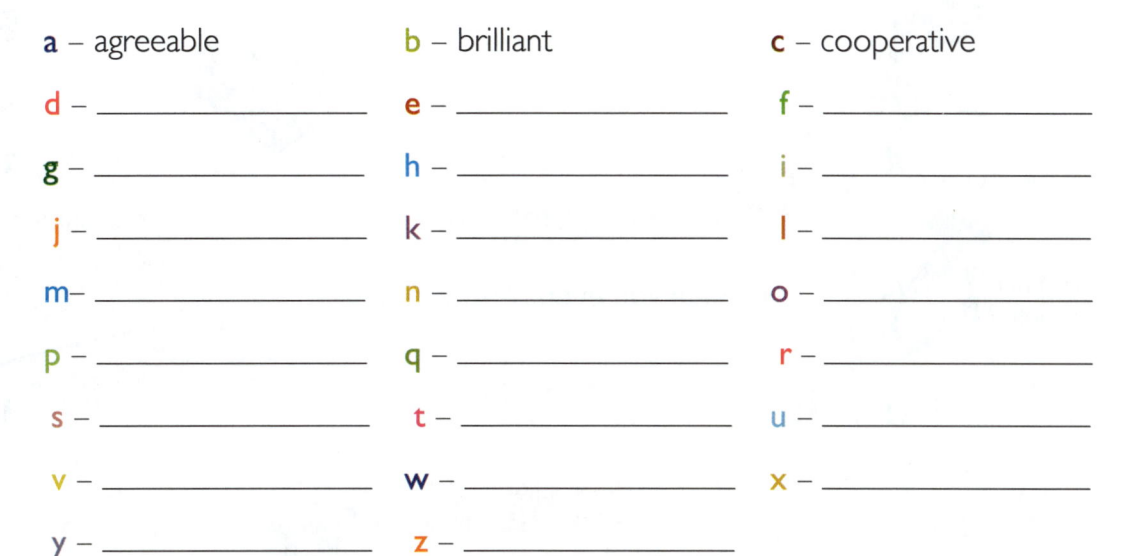

   a – agreeable   b – brilliant   c – cooperative
   d – _____   e – _____   f – _____
   g – _____   h – _____   i – _____
   j – _____   k – _____   l – _____
   m – _____   n – _____   o – _____
   p – _____   q – _____   r – _____
   s – _____   t – _____   u – _____
   v – _____   w – _____   x – _____
   y – _____   z – _____

   b) Think about a list of positive verbs. There are three examples for you.

   a – appreciate   b – build   c – create
   d – _____   e – _____   f – _____
   g – _____   h – _____   i – _____
   j – _____   k – _____   l – _____
   m – _____   n – _____   o – _____
   p – _____   q – _____   r – _____
   s – _____   t – _____   u – _____
   v – _____   w – _____   x – _____
   y – _____   z – _____

   c) In your notebook write sentences or create expressions with the words from the exercises "a" and "b". Exchange lists in class.

   d) Select which list was the most creative.

Let's have fun!

let's play the present perfect board game!

5 Have you ever met twins?

6 How long have you lived in your city / town?

7 Go back 2 spaces

8 Have you received a gift this month?

9 Have you ever eaten feijoada?

4 Have you ever lived in another country?

Remember that:
- Have you ever...? (questions)

10 Have you eaten in a restaurant this week?

3 Miss a turn!

- **For**: duration of an action
- **Since**: moment when an action started

FINISH

11 Move forward 3 spaces

2 How long have you studied English?

12 How long have you lived in Brazil?

- **Already**: Affirmative sentences
- **Yet**: Questions and negative sentences

18 Have you ever been to Rio?

1 Have you ever skied?

17 Have you ever climbed a mountain?

13 Have you ever had a tattoo?

START

16 Have you visited your grandparents recently?

15 Miss a turn!

14 Have you done your homework yet?

80

Exercise the mind

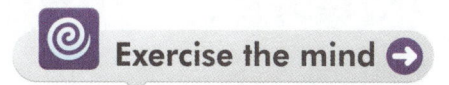

WARM-UP: Many financial analysts say Brazil is the country of the present. Brazilian magazines also state that Brazil is the country of the present. What about you? Do you believe this?

1. Look at this Brazilian magazine. What's the headline?

2. What have you done as a Brazilian citizen to be part of this growing country?

SPECIAL EDITION IN ENGLISH

EXAME

30/12/2010 N°2 www.exame.com.br R$ 29,90

Brazil, the country of the present

The main articles of EXAME about Brazil in 2010

- The new middle class
- The demographics of growth
- The decade of infrastructure begins
- The power of the female consumer
- The Brazilian stock market
- The Chinese are already here

- Are you from the new middle class?
- Do you have female consumers in your family?
- Do you know what the stock market is?
- Search for Chinese people in Brazil.

3. You are a Brazilian citizen. What have you done to become a world citizen?

UNIT 8

INTERNATIONAL ENGLISH

- Plays – Playwrights – Relative pronouns

WARM-UP: Do you like plays?

Have you ever acted in a play?

Would you like to be an actor / an actress?

Read

1. Read the play below.

FASHION

CHARACTERS	Millionaires 1 and 2 Designers 1 to 3

DESIGNER 1	Hurry up!
DESIGNER 2	I'm getting ready!
DESIGNER 3	What time is it?
DESIGNER 1	It's three-thirty.
DESIGNER 2	Oh, my God!
DESIGNER 3	Hurry up! Hurry up!
DESIGNER 1	The millionaires are coming.
DESIGNER 2	We're late!
DESIGNER 3	We're very, very late!
DESIGNER 1	Where are the pictures?
DESIGNER 2	(*Showing.*) They're here.
DESIGNER 3	I hope they like our clothes.
DESIGNER 1	(*Pointing.*) Look! Here they come!

(The millionaires enter.)

MILLIONAIRE 1	Good afternoon!
DESIGNER 2	Good afternoon!
MILLIONAIRE 2	We want to see beautiful clothes!
DESIGNER 3	Yes, of course!
MILLIONAIRE 1	Money is not important.
MILLIONAIRE 2	We're millionaires!
MILLIONAIRE 1	We won the Mega Sena![1]
MILLIONAIRE 2	We are very very rich!
DESIGNER 1	Sure.
DESIGNER 2	What are you looking for?
MILLIONAIRE 1	The latest fashion!
MILLIONAIRE 2	We're millionaires!
MILLIONAIRE 1	We have to be elegant!
MILLIONAIRE 2	Very very elegant!
DESIGNER 3	Right! Let's start the fashion show!
DESIGNER 1	(*Showing a picture.*) Look at this dress! It's beautiful!
MILLIONAIRE 1	It's too simple! I'm a millionaire.
DESIGNER 2	(*Showing a picture.*) Look at these pants. They're very chic.
MILLIONAIRE 2	They're chic for you! Not for millionaires like us!
MILLIONAIRE 1	We are very very rich!
DESIGNER 3	(*Showing a picture.*) Do you like these shoes? They're elegant!
MILLIONAIRE 2	They're ugly!
MILLIONAIRE 1	We want beautiful things.
MILLIONAIRE 2	We're millionaires!
MILLIONAIRE 1	We're very very rich!
DESIGNER 1	I understand that!
DESIGNER 2	(*Showing a picture.*) Look at this marvelous sweater!
MILLIONAIRE 2	Marvelous? It's terrible.
MILLIONAIRE 1	Look. We're...
DESIGNER 3	(*Interrupting.*) Millionaires! You're very very very rich! I know!

1. The Mega Sena is a famous lottery in Brazil.

MILLIONAIRE 2	That's right.
MILLIONAIRE 1	Show us the fashion!
DESIGNER 1	(*Showing a picture.*) How about this T-shirt?
DESIGNER 2	(*Showing a picture.*) This skirt?
DESIGNER 3	(*Showing a picture.*) These shorts?
DESIGNER 1	(*Showing a picture.*) These socks?
MILLIONAIRE 2	Stop!
MILLIONAIRE 1	That's enough!
MILLIONAIRE 2	Your clothes are awful!
MILLIONAIRE 1	You are offending us!
MILLIONAIRE 2	We're milionaires!
MILLIONAIRE 1	We are…
DESIGNER 2	(*Interrupting.*) Very very rich! I know!
MILLIONAIRE 2	Let's get out of here!
MILLIONAIRE 1	Yes. Let's go to "Saslú."[2]
DESIGNER 3	Wait! Don't go!
MILLIONAIRE 2	Why not?
DESIGNER 1	Before you go, let us copy your clothes!
DESIGNER 2	They're very elegant and chic.
MILLIONAIRE 1	Do you think so?
DESIGNER 3	Of course!
DESIGNER 1	We can use them to start a new collection!
MILLIONAIRE 2	Hey, I'm starting to like this place!
MILLIONAIRE 1	Yes, me too.
MILLIONAIRE 2	They know a lot about fashion!
DESIGNER 2	(*To the other designers.*) Well, we know a lot about psychology!
DESIGNER 3	That's right!

(*They all laugh.*)

2. You can use the name of a very fashionable store in your city.

THE END

From GONTOW, Carlos. The classroom is a stage. São Paulo: Disal Editora, 2005.

2. **You can act out this play in groups. Let's check what you need.**

   a) How many characters?
   5 characters.

   b) Who are they?

   c) Where do you think this story is happening?

   d) What do you need to perform this play?

   e) Who else is necessary to help in the play?

   f) Now it's your turn. Come on and demonstrate your acting skills. Organize your groups. Work with these subjects and act out the play: characters, action, and setting.

Listen

1. The students are in the Use of Technology class. They are in the computer lab. They are learning how to design a website. The website is about William Shakespeare, one of the greatest poets and playwrights of all times.

   TRACK 20

2. Read the dialogue below. Number the steps in the corresponding sequence you hear.

   Mrs. Costa is talking to the students.

   Mrs. Costa: I would like to suggest a few tips when you create or design a website.

   (   ) Include resources besides the one you are creating so that other students keep on discovering new things about the topic;

   (1) Design a mind gap about Shakespeare. Write down as many ideas as you can about the website you want to create;

   (   ) Try to limit each section of the website to two pages of A4;

   (   ) Next, do some research about the resources that might be available to support your ideas;

   (   ) Start working good luck!

   (   ) Try to write short, concise paragraphs;

84

Speak

1. The students are researching Shakespeare's life. They have found pictures and subtitles. Help them match the pictures and the corresponding paragraphs. Work in pairs or in groups.

a)

b)

c)

d)

e)

(   ) They had three children: Susana who was born in 1583, and the twins, Hamnet and Judith who where born in 1585.

(a) William Shakespeare was born in Stratford--upon-Avon on April 23rd, 1564. He was the third of eight children. Stratford-upon--Avon is where he grew up.

(   ) When King James came to the throne in 1603, he chose Shakespeare's group of actors to be his royal entertainers. They were called "The King's Men" and they performed plays in his honor.

(   ) On November 28th, 1582, Shakespeare married Anne Hathaway, who was eight years older than him.

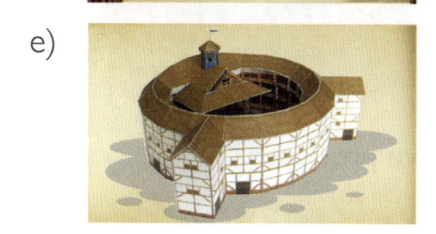

(   ) The acting troupe needed a playhouse to perform their plays. The Globe Theater was not only one of the most famous playhouses of all time, but the playhouse where Shakespeare performed many of his greatest plays.

Click

<www.shakespeareglobe.com>. Acesso em: 13 dez. 2011.
Site do Teatro Globe em Londres.

Don't miss!

SHAPIRO, James. **1599 – Um Ano na Vida de William Shakespeare**. São Paulo: Planeta, 2011.

Grammar points

1. Read the sentences taken from the previous page about Shakespeare.

- Shakespeare married Anne Hathaway **who** was eight years older than him.
- Stratford-upon-Avon is **where** Shakespeare grew up.

Who and where are relative pronouns. In the sentences above they were used to combine two related ideas together.

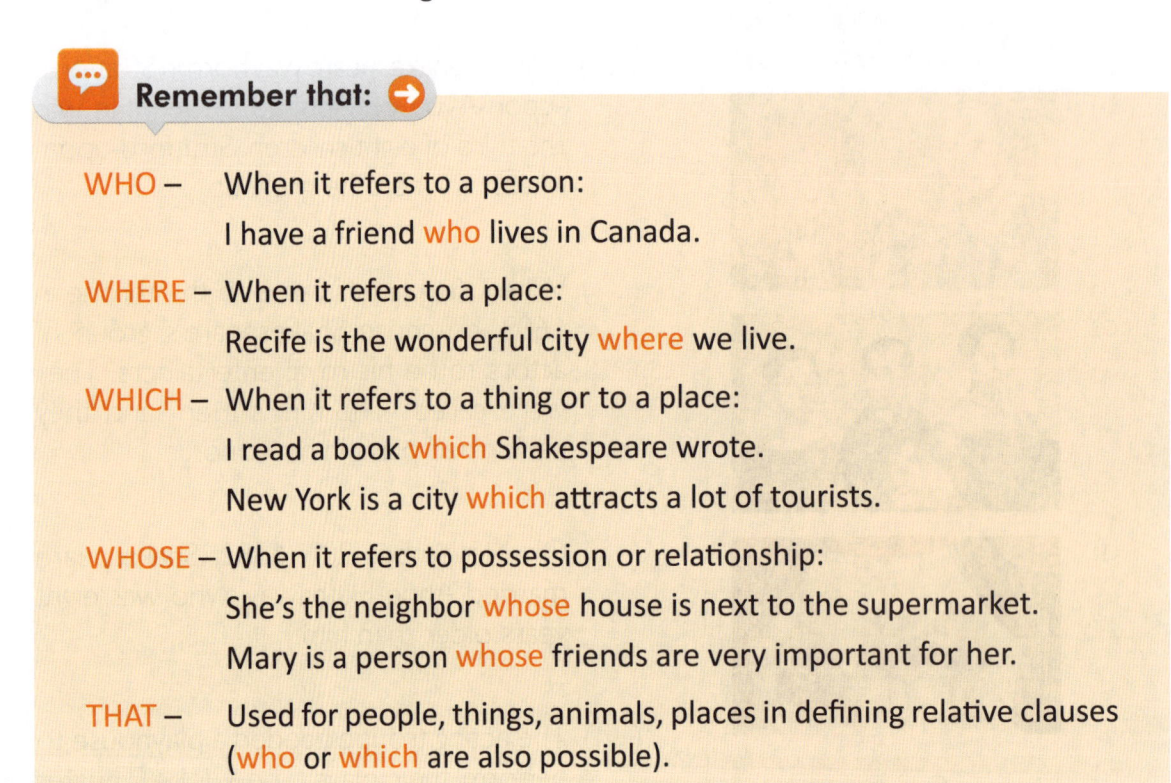

Remember that:

WHO – When it refers to a person:
I have a friend who lives in Canada.

WHERE – When it refers to a place:
Recife is the wonderful city where we live.

WHICH – When it refers to a thing or to a place:
I read a book which Shakespeare wrote.
New York is a city which attracts a lot of tourists.

WHOSE – When it refers to possession or relationship:
She's the neighbor whose house is next to the supermarket.
Mary is a person whose friends are very important for her.

THAT – Used for people, things, animals, places in defining relative clauses (who or which are also possible).

2. Complete the sentences. Use the correct relative pronouns.

a) I told you about **who** lives here.

b) My cat, _____ is white, is very nice.

c) Do you know the boy _____ mother is a teacher?

d) This is the store in _____ I bought my dress.

e) That is my friend Kate _____ works at school.

f) That's the house _____ I grew up.

g) The film, _____ I didn't like, won an award.

h) My neighbor, _____ works with me, is from Ceará.

Vocabulary

1. What is a friend? Can you describe what a real friend is? Read the quotations. Which one do you like most?

> All people want is someone to listen.
>
> (Hugh Elliot)

> In prosperity our friends know us, in adversity we know our friends.
>
> (John Churton Collins)

From: <www.quotationspage.com/subjects/friendship/>. Accessed on: December 13th, 2011.

2. Complete the questionnaire. Check all the items that you believe are true for you.

A friend is someone who...

a) ( ) cries with and for you.
b) ( ) does the homework for you.
c) ( ) lends you money.
d) ( ) keeps your secrets.
e) ( ) respects you.
f) ( ) understands and supports you.
g) ( ) talks to you everyday.
h) ( ) always tells you the truth.
i) ( ) accepts you the way you are.
j) ( ) _____
k) ( ) _____
l) ( ) _____

3. Discuss the reasons for your choices.

A: I don't agree. A friend is someone who doesn't let you cry.

B: I think a friend is someone who cries with you.

Click

<http://www.poemsonly.com/category/friendshippoems.php>. Acesso em: 23 fev. 2012.
Site com poemas em inglês sobre amizade.

Write

Designing a website

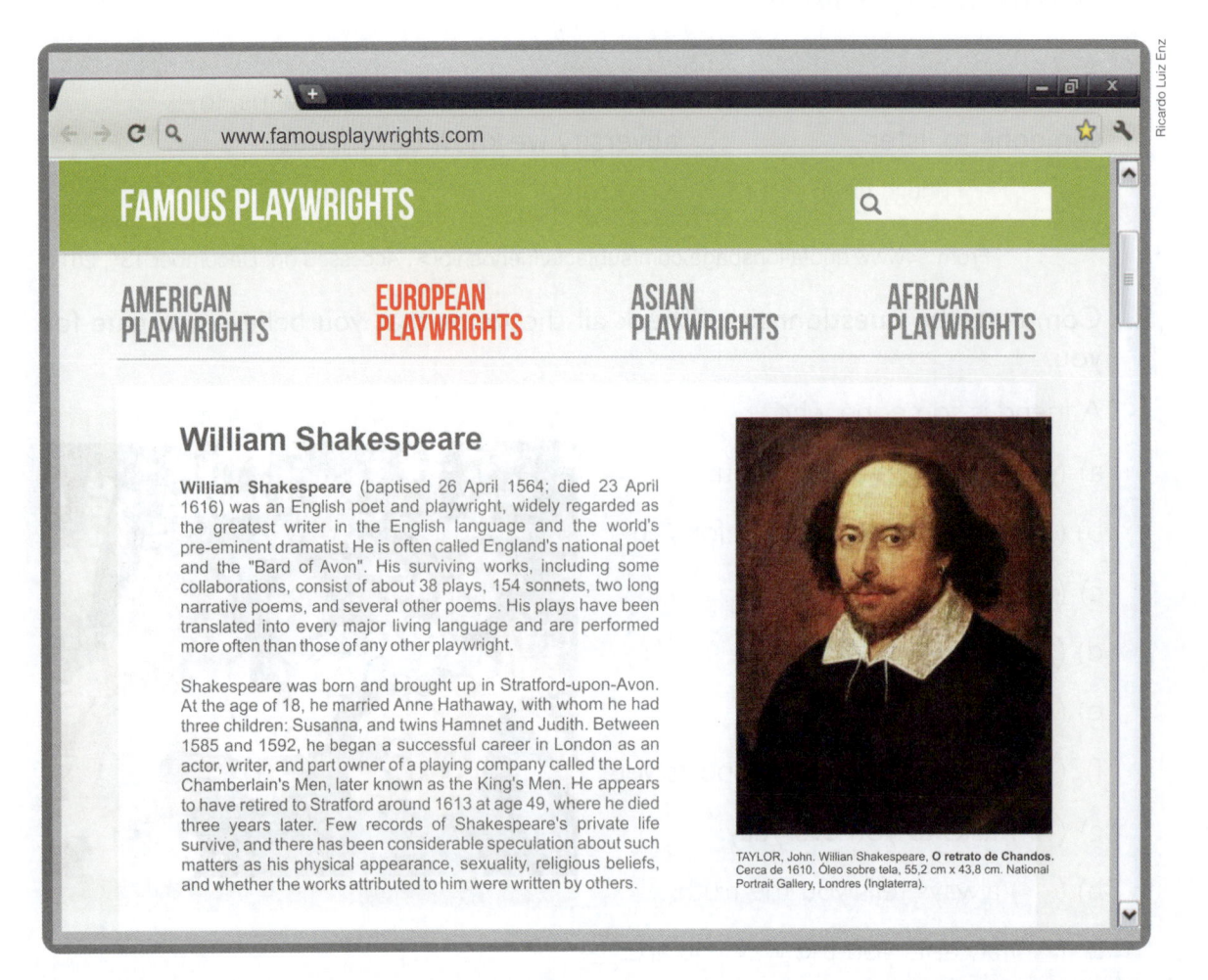

FAMOUS PLAYWRIGHTS

www.famousplaywrights.com

AMERICAN PLAYWRIGHTS | EUROPEAN PLAYWRIGHTS | ASIAN PLAYWRIGHTS | AFRICAN PLAYWRIGHTS

William Shakespeare

William Shakespeare (baptised 26 April 1564; died 23 April 1616) was an English poet and playwright, widely regarded as the greatest writer in the English language and the world's pre-eminent dramatist. He is often called England's national poet and the "Bard of Avon". His surviving works, including some collaborations, consist of about 38 plays, 154 sonnets, two long narrative poems, and several other poems. His plays have been translated into every major living language and are performed more often than those of any other playwright.

Shakespeare was born and brought up in Stratford-upon-Avon. At the age of 18, he married Anne Hathaway, with whom he had three children: Susanna, and twins Hamnet and Judith. Between 1585 and 1592, he began a successful career in London as an actor, writer, and part owner of a playing company called the Lord Chamberlain's Men, later known as the King's Men. He appears to have retired to Stratford around 1613 at age 49, where he died three years later. Few records of Shakespeare's private life survive, and there has been considerable speculation about such matters as his physical appearance, sexuality, religious beliefs, and whether the works attributed to him were written by others.

TAYLOR, John. Willian Shakespeare, **O retrato de Chandos**. Cerca de 1610. Óleo sobre tela, 55,2 cm x 43,8 cm. National Portrait Gallery, Londres (Inglaterra).

1. **What you need to prepare your website.**

   - Work in pairs or in groups. You're going to create a website about a famous Brazilian playwright;

   - Look at the webpage above. Does it have any links? What are they? In your opinion who are the other playwrights?

   - In your group make a list of the most famous Brazilian playwrights.

   - You can design different links for playwrights from different Brazilian states or regions.

   - After you have chosen a Brazilian playwright, write down some notes. Think of what may be interesting to talk about. Remember that you need to call the reader's attention.

2. What you need to make your website.

- Write a short text about the Brazilian playwright you have already chosen. Add your notes.

- When the text is finished, read it through again. Think about what you can improve. Underline words, check punctuation and correct miswritten words. Use a dictionary. Discuss the correction. Rewrite the text.

- Look for pictures which are related to your text from magazines, newspapers or the internet. Pick up a piece of paper. Put all the texts and the pictures and arrange them so that all your classmates can see which texts belong to the links you have created.

- Now it's time to go to the computer lab and finish your website including the texts and pictures about the playwrights.

- At the end, compare different webpages with different Brazilian playwrights.

3. Here are some suggestions for your website. They are famous Brazilian playwrights.

BERNARDELLI, Henrique. **Machado de Assis**. Cerca de 1905. Óleo sobre tela. Academia Brasileira de Letras, Rio de Janeiro (RJ).

Machado de Assis

Maria Clara Machado

Janete Clair

Benedito Ruy Barbosa

Let's have fun!

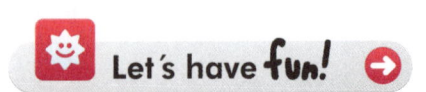

WARM-UP: What kind of English do you speak?

Do you speak American English? British English? Or a different variety?

1. 17th Century

In 1620 a group of people sailed from England to North America. These people spoke English and they were very religious. They spoke Shakespeare's language. It was very different from modern English. These immigrants needed new words for animals and plants they had never seen before and they used native American words for them. American English was becoming different from the English the pilgrims spoke in England.

2. 18th Century

After the USA became independent from England (1776), there were many other influences in the English language: French spoken in Louisiana, Spanish spoken in the colonies in the South. They also invented new words for their lives in the USA. Another important influence was the language spoken by the slaves. In 1885 Mark Twain wrote Huckleberry Finn where he used this language in it.

Why are there different types of English?

THE STORY OF ENGLISH

Because of:
- History
- Geography
- Politics
- Social Economic issues and interests

4. 20th and 21st century

Because of the invention of the cinema, American English was heard in Britain, and it started changing British English. British and American English became closer in many ways. Today we know that theater (AE) and theatre (BE), apartment (AE) and flat (BE) are the same words. British English has also influenced Asian music and Bollywood movies in India. Asian English is now part of General British.
Movies spread American English all around the word. Today English is spoken as a 1st, 2nd or foreign language. Non-native speakers of English use English as an international language of communication.

3. 19th and 20th century

Many immigrants went to the USA in both centuries. They came from different countries and they wanted to start a new life in the USA. They were from Japan, Russia, Italy, China, Spain, Mexico and they all contributed with new words and expressions to American English. Speaking of Britain, the British Empire expanded its power to its colonies: India, Australia, Asia, New England and Africa. British English became the language of the government. New varieties of English appeared. Indian English, Australian English, South African English, etc…

5. CONCLUSION

There are many different varieties of English. English is an international language and it belongs to the world. All types of English are correct. What about you? Are there many varieties of Portuguese? What kind of Portuguese do you speak?

Exercise the mind

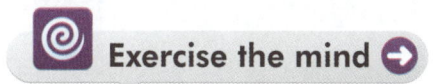

1. Do a class survey. Write about your classmates.

NAME	SOME ADJECTIVES WHICH DESCRIBE MY CLASSMATES' PERSONALITIES
José	is generous. He gives his friend his time.
Maria Eduarda	is honest. She always tells the truth.
Felipe	is funny. He makes me laugh.
Amanda	is hard-working. She studies a lot.

2. Think about other adjectives to describe your classmates.

   - Friendly: is nice to people; shows interest and goodwill.
   - Sympathetic: understands people's problems.
   - Outgoing: openly friendly; extroverted.

3. Collect the information from exercises 1 and 2. Take a picture of your friends and make a poster about your friends' personalities.

Now it's your turn.

Provide a picture of your friends and make your poster. Choose the most creative poster.

Review 4: UNIT 7/8

1. **Answer these personal questions.**

   a) Have you ever thought about living in New Zealand?
   _____

   b) Have you ever dreamed of UFOs?
   _____

   c) How long have you lived in your city?
   _____

   d) Have you watched any rock shows recently? If yes, which one(s)?
   _____

   e) Have you watched any horror movies recently?
   _____

2. **Complete the sentences with for or since.**

   a) I've lived in Curitiba **since** 1982.

   b) They haven't traveled _____ March.

   c) My dog has been sick _____ two days.

   d) I have studied English _____ five months.

   e) My daughter has been vegetarian _____ last summer.

   f) Craig has lived in South Africa _____ he was born.

   g) The students have wanted to see this movie _____ three weeks.

   h) They have known each other _____ years.

3. **Match the adjectives and their corresponding definitions:**

   a) Hard-working   (   ) tells the truth.
   b) Honest   (   ) understands people's problems.
   c) Outgoing   (   ) is nice to new people.
   d) Sympathetic   (   ) is liberal with giving and sharing.
   e) Funny   (a) is dedicated to work and study.
   f) Generous   (   ) is openly friendly.
   g) Friendly   (   ) makes you laugh.

4. WHO, WHICH, or WHOSE?

a) She likes hamburgers **which** are spicy.

b) Can I talk to the girl _____ is standing in line?

c) That is the man _____ had a car accident.

d) I haven't seen my neighbor, _____ house is next to my house, for a long time.

e) Yesterday my father saw a car _____ he liked very much.

5. Read the paragraphs on page 85 about Shakespeare. Are the sentences below True (T) or False (F) according to the paragraphs?

a) Shakespeare was born in Stratford-upon-Avon. (**T**)

b) He grew up in London. ( )

c) He married Anne Hathway. ( )

d) The Globe Theater was a playhouse where Shakespeare performed many of his plays. ( )

e) He had four sons and didn't have any daughters. ( )

6. Draw a detached house. In your drawing include:
- two floors   – six windows   – two doors   – a garage for two cars
  – a front garden with two trees

Click

<http://www.chriton.com/english/glossary/detached.htm>. Acesso em: 23 fev. 2012.
Site com modelos de *detached houses*.

Workbook

Unit 1

1. Read the text.

Earth is the third planet from the Sun. It is also the fifth largest planet in our solar system. Our planet is the only one in our solar system where there is liquid water.

The atmosphere on Earth is composed of nitrogen, oxygen, carbon dioxide and some other gases. Life on Earth is only possible due to this mix of liquid water and atmosphere.

The Earth orbits around the Sun once every 365 days and rotates on its axis once every 24 hours. This rotation is what causes day and night. Because Earth's axis is tilted a little bit, there is also a change of seasons.

There are volcanoes, mountains and valleys on Earth like Mars and Venus. Our planet has only one naturally occurring satellite, the Moon. From Earth, you can see only one side of the moon.

2. Look at the pictures and match.

The Sun   The Moon   Mars   ~~Venus~~

a) Venus

b)

c)

d)

3. Answer the questions about the text.

   a) Why is life possible on Earth?
   Because of the mix between liquid water and atmosphere.

   b) What is the atmosphere of Earth composed of?
   _____

   c) Where does the Earth orbit around?
   _____

   d) When does the Earth rotate on its axis?
   _____

   e) Are there any volcanoes, mountains and valleys on Earth? Where else?
   _____

   f) What is our planet's satellite? _____

4. Look at the verbs below.

   decompose/produce/refrigerate/plant/deforest

5. When we add –ion or –tion to the verbs, it changes the meaning the word. See how to change the verb by adding the suffix –ion or –tion: decompose/decomposition. Look for the other 4 words modified by the suffixes.

D	W	R	T	C	M	J	S	D	A	Y	D	F	G	H	C	N	M	F
E	A	S	D	F	T	G	H	J	H	K	L	L	H	D	C	S	D	Q
C	C	R	E	F	R	I	G	E	R	A	T	I	O	N	H	C	E	W
O	S	D	V	E	H	J	J	F	C	K	L	M	M	E	J	V	F	E
M	F	G	A	Z	X	V	B	M	N	C	M	V	N	U	N	M	O	R
P	N	R	S	E	R	T	I	H	F	S	A	L	M	T	O	H	R	G
O	A	A	M	A	J	F	H	T	D	A	Y	H	S	H	I	U	E	Y
S	G	L	L	G	S	H	A	F	D	Q	W	V	H	D	T	S	S	U
I	F	G	N	O	I	T	C	U	D	O	R	P	D	G	A	C	T	I
T	F	H	L	A	S	G	J	H	K	M	Q	W	E	H	T	V	A	O
I	S	D	F	G	S	J	M	F	L	Y	I	M	V	H	N	B	T	P
O	S	D	H	J	E	N	J	K	L	M	N	M	G	T	A	N	I	L
N	H	M	K	M	E	R	H	J	G	J	S	N	D	H	L	M	O	H
A	S	F	G	J	K	U	D	S	L	A	R	H	V	L	P	K	N	J
F	X	N	J	C	F	W	S	D	F	S	G	M	D	K	S	K	D	K
W	C	S	V	F	J	T	K	F	M	F	D	S	R	M	S	D	F	K

95

Unit 2

1. Complete the sentences with the comparative form of the adjectives.

   a) Canada is **larger** than Cuba. (large)

   b) English is _____ than Arabic. (easy)

   c) Nancy's hair is _____ than Julia's hair. (short)

   d) This dress is _____ than my mother's dress. (expensive)

   e) Pasta is _____ than fish. (good)

   f) Soccer is _____ than handball. (popular)

2. Label the weather. Write the comparative form of the adjectives.

   a) sunny – sunnier than

   b) _____

   c) _____

   d) _____

   e) _____

   f) _____

3. Match the natural disasters and the corresponding definitions.

a) hurricane
b) drought
c) earthquake
d) flood
e) tsunami
f) landslide
g) blizzard

Australia, 2010.

( ) A great sea wave produced by submarine earth movement or volcanic eruption.

(a) A tropical cyclone with winds usually accompanied by, rain, thunder and lightning.

( ) A long severe snowstorm.

( ) A rapid downward movement of a mass of rock, earth or artificial fill on a slope.

( ) A shaking or trembling of the earth that is volcanic or tectonic in origin.

( ) A rising and overflowing of a body of water onto normally dry land.

( ) A period of dryness especially when prolonged.

4. Gabriela, Cate, Lyndon and Kazuki are at the Physical Education class now. Look at their measurements.

	Gabriela	Cate	Lyndon	Kazuki
AGE	14	13	14	13
HEIGHT	1.68	1.65	1.75	1.70
WEIGHT	57 kilos	59 kilos	60 kilos	55 kilos

a) Cate / Kazuki (tall): **Kazuki is taller than Cate.**

b) Lyndon / Gabriela (old): _____

c) Gabriela / Cate (old): _____

d) Kazuki / Lyndon (heavy): _____

Review → **Unit 1/2**

1. Write sentences. Follow the model.

   a) In the / science class / The students / now / are

   The students are in the science class now.

   b) the greenhouse effect / about / Ricardo / knows

   _____

   c) the effects of / Gabriela / global warming / talks about

   _____

   d) in the planet's average surface temperature / Global warming / an increase / refers to

   _____

   e) an increase / The main greenhouse gases / in the average global temperature / contribute to

   _____

2. Now write the sentences from exercise 1 in the Simple Past tense.

   a) **The students were in the science class.**

   b) _____

   c) _____

   d) _____

   e) _____

98

3. Complete the chart with the missing comparative and superlative forms of the adjectives.

ADJECTIVE	COMPARATIVE	SUPERLATIVE
fat	fatter than	the fattest
hot		
old		
interesting	more interesting than	the most interesting
expensive		
tall		
long		
popular		
easy		

Check List – Things I can do in English

☺ I can.

😐 I don't think I can.

☹ I can't. I want to review.

☐ Using the Simple Present.

☐ Comparative Forms: Comparing things, places and people.

☐ Using the Simple Past.

☐ Superlative Forms: Comparing things, places and people.

☐ Talking about global warming and the greenhouse effect.

☐ Talking about natural disasters.

Unit 3

1. **Look at the examples and complete the explanations.**

PRESENT (TO HAVE)	
I have	
You have	
He has	
She has	to study for the test.
It has	
We have	
You have	
They have	

   a) We use **has to** or _____ + verb to describe rules or obligations.

   b) **Have to** and _____ mean that something is necessary:
   I'm late! I have to go.
   I'm late! I must go.

2. **Now let's put "have to" in the negative form in the Simple Present. Complete.**

   I don't have
   _____
   He doesn't have
   _____ to wake up early in the morning.
   It doesn't have
   We don't have
   You don't have
   _____

   a) We use _____ or _____ + verb to say that something is not necessary. There's a choice.

   b) We use _____ to describe a prohibition. There aren't any choices.
   You mustn't drive without a driving license.
   Don't drive without a driving license.

3. **Complete the sentences. Use has to or have to and the verbs from the box.**

   wear – ~~stay~~ – work – go – clear

   a) I go out on Saturdays but during the week **I have to stay** at home.

b) It's too late. She _____ right now.

c) The students at school _____ uniforms.

d) Gabriela _____ the table after dinner.

e) My mother is a nurse. Sometimes she _____ at night.

4. Pretend you're in Paris. Here are some tips for tourists. Complete the sentences with **should** or **shouldn't**.

   a) You **should** visit the Eiffel Tower.

   b) You _____ try to get a plane without a ticket.

   c) You _____ put your money in your wallet, not in the back pocket of your jeans.

   d) You _____ go out without a raincoat. It usually rains in the afternoon.

   e) You _____ cover your guidebook so you don't look like a tourist.

5. Match the examples.

   a) I can help old people and young children.
   b) I can't go far away. We have to stop here.
   c) I could ride a horse when I was 10.
   d) We could talk a lot here but now it's not allowed.

   (   ) Ability in the past   (   ) Permission in the present
   (a) Ability in the present   (   ) Permission in the past

6. Circle the correct opinions.

   a) A: Take your umbrella. It should / (might) rain this afternoon.
      B: Really? The weather forecast was for sun.

   b) A: May / Must I come in?
      B: Yes, sure!

   c) A: Tomorrow I should / might go to the beach, but I'm not sure.
      B: OK, but if you decide to go, call me.

   d) A: Where's Eddie?
      B: I don't know. He may / has to be on vacation.

Unit 4

1. Label the pictures. Use the phrasal verbs below.

   take off his cap
   put on his sneakers
   put away his books
   call up her mom
   turn on the TV
   throw away the paper

   a)  **Turn on the TV**
   b)  _____
   c)  _____
   d)  _____
   e)  _____
   f) _____

2. Look at the invitation below for Laura's party. Write questions and answers about the invitation.

   You are invited to a birthday party!
   FOR: Laura
   PLACE: 15, Big Wood Avenue
   DATE: Friday, November 30th
   TIME: 7:00 – 10:00 p.m.
   We'll have pizza, soda and cake
   PLEASE CALL: 3242-1740
   COME AND JOIN US!

   a) WHERE
   Where will the party be?
   It will be at 15, Big Wood Avenue.

   b) WHEN
   _____

   c) WHAT TIME / START
   _____

   d) WHAT TIME / END
   _____

   e) WHAT FOOD AND DRINK / SERVE
   _____

3. Complete the dialogue with the correct forms of **will** and the verbs in parentheses. Use contractions when possible.

Server: Hello, guys. Are you ready to order?

Gabriela: I think so… I'm really hungry. I**'ll have** a chicken sandwich and orange juice.
(have)

David: I'm hungry too but I _____ any chicken. I'_____
(not eat)   (have)
a mixed green salad, a ham and cheese sandwich, and a soda.

Kazuki: I think I'_____ some pasta. Yes, I'_____ lasagna.
(choose)   (eat)

Server: Ok, thank you. I'_____ back in ten minutes with your orders.
(be)

4. By the years 2050 what do you think the world will be like? Write five sentences using <u>will</u>. There's one example for you.

Ex.: **Private planes will be common.**

a) _____

b) _____

c) _____

d) _____

e) _____

Review — Unit 3/4

1. Write sentences. Say what you **must** or **mustn't** do in your school.

- Eat in the classroom
- Respect teachers and classmates
- Leave the classroom without permission
- Use your cellphone
- Listen to music

_____

_____

_____

_____

2. Draw a line between the traffic signs and its corresponding meaning.

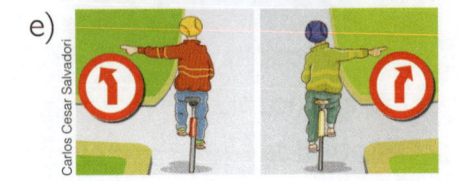

a)

b)

c)

d)

e)

No pets

STOP

Pedestrian crossing

You must signal when you turn left or right

Handicapped

3. Write the corresponding **phrasal verbs** under the corresponding column.

your sneakers – the TV – your homework – the computer – your brother – your cap – the radio – your coat – the lights – your friends – your watch – your composition – the CD player – your shoes – your parents – the cellphone

Turn on / Turn off	Put on / Take off	Call up	Hand in
the TV			

4. Unscramble the words and write sentences.

a) throw away / will / the paper / Gabriela.
   Gabriela will throw away the paper.

b) be / crowded / The world / won't /.
   _____

c) she / in the minutes / Will / be back / ?
   _____

d) how to grow food / We / know / in the ocean / will / .
   _____

Check List – Things I can do in English

☺ I can.

😐 I don't think I can.

☹ I can't. I want to review.

- ☐ Recognizing traffic signs.
- ☐ Talking about rules.
- ☐ Expressing ability and asking for permission.
- ☐ Expressing possibility.
- ☐ Expressing obligation and prohibition.
- ☐ Reflecting about bullying and the effects it can have on people.
- ☐ Making predictions.
- ☐ Talking about the future.
- ☐ Using phrasal verbs.

Unit 5

1. **Choose the best ending for each sentence.**

   a) Gabriela was watching TV when…
   - ( ) the lights went out.
   - ( ) the lights go out.
   - ( ) the lights were going out.

   b) Kazuki was reading his geography book when…
   - ( ) Mrs. Weber was walking into the classroom.
   - ( ) Mrs. Weber walked into the classroom.
   - ( ) Mrs. Weber walks into the classroom.

   c) Laura and Ricardo were riding their bikes when…
   - ( ) Sarah calls up.
   - ( ) Sarah was calling up.
   - ( ) Sarah called up.

   d) Mrs. Weber was checking homework when…
   - ( ) Cate went to the girls' room.
   - ( ) Cate goes to the girls' room.
   - ( ) Cate was going to the girls' room.

2. **Copy the parts of the sentences into the corresponding columns.**

	SHORT ACTION	LONGER ACTION
a)	The lights went out	when Gabriela was watching TV.
b)		
c)		
d)		

3. What were the students doing yesterday at 5 p.m?
Look at the pictures and answer the questions.

a) Was Cate doing homework?
   No, she wasn't.

b) What was Cate doing?
   _____

c) Was Ricardo playing soccer?
   _____

d) Were Kazuki and David eating?
   _____

e) What were Kazuki and David doing?
   _____

4. Complete the questions with the Past Progressive. Then write short answers.

a) **Were you studying** (you / study) last night?
   Yes, I was / No, I wasn't.

b) What _____ (you / do) on Saturday evening?
   _____

c) Where _____ (you / go) this morning?
   _____

d) _____ (you / watch TV) one hour ago?
   _____

107

Unit 6

1. Can you find the Past Participle of irregular verbs in your English-Portuguese dictionary? Look at this example. Find the Past Participle of the following verbs in your dictionary:

   go verbo, substantivo

   → Verbo intransitivo (3ª Pessoa singular presente **goes**; pretérito **went**, particípio passado **gone**

	INFINITIVE	PAST FORM	PAST PARTICIPLE
a	go	went	gone
b	do		
c	drink		
d	know		
e	spend		
f	buy		
g	live		
h	work		
i	swim		
j	grow		

2. Now complete the sentences with the verbs in parentheses in the Present Perfect form:

   a) Ricardo **has gone** out for some coffee. (go)

   b) _____ Gabriela _____ the air plane ticket? (buy)

   c) My cat _____ never _____ milk. Can you believe it? (drink)

   d) My parents _____ for ten years. They're retired. (work)

   e) _____ Kazuki and his family ever _____ in Japan?

3. Write sentences. Use <u>never</u> or <u>ever</u>.

a) She / study / Italian?

Has she ever studied Italian?

b) We / drink / pineapple juice (X)

_____

c) You / eat / Chinese food?

_____

d) They / speak / Portuguese/

_____

e) My grandparents / visit / London (X)

_____

4. Write questions for the answers.

a) **Have you played volleyball this term?**

No, I haven't played volleyball this term.

b) _____

No, she hasn't slept well.

c) _____

No, we haven't baked cookies.

d) _____

No, they haven't gone fishing.

e) _____

No, he hasn't cheated on the math test.

f) _____

No, you haven't flown in a balloon.

Review — Unit 5/6

1. Complete the sentences. What were the students doing when the bell rang?

a) **Kazuki was eating a sandwich.**

b) _____

c) _____

d) _____

e) _____

2. Find and search the verbs in the Past Participle in the wordsearch. Then, write them.

E	A	T	E	N	A	D	T	D	L	L	B	E	E	N	S
A	B	A	A	S	F	A	M	F	Q	G	L	J	O	D	H
S	S	V	A	V	M	H	L	C	H	E	A	T	E	D	H
A	F	B	A	K	E	D	J	K	N	D	K	H	D	S	R
G	F	G	I	Z	X	V	B	C	N	F	F	H	J	S	J
O	N	D	D	E	R	T	I	H	F	L	A	L	M	L	E
N	A	E	M	A	T	O	L	D	D	O	Y	H	S	E	H
E	G	S	L	G	S	E	E	N	D	W	W	V	H	P	J
D	F	U	H	E	A	R	D	A	R	N	V	M	H	T	S
Q	F	H	L	S	P	O	K	E	N	M	H	I	N	K	H
V	P	E	N	T	S	S	M	F	L	Y	I	B	V	H	U
E	S	D	H	J	E	A	V	W	R	I	T	T	E	N	F

eat – **eaten**
see – _____
be – _____
go – _____
fly – _____
sleep – _____
cheat – _____
speak – _____
write – _____
have – _____
use – _____

Check List – Things I can do in English

☺ I can.

😐 I don't think I can.

☹ I can't. I want to review.

☐ Use the Past Progressive: talking about actions that were in progress at a specific time.

☐ Using Simple Past for shorter actions and the Past Progressive for longer actions.

☐ Writing a short biography in English.

☐ Talking about Kwanzaa.

☐ Using the Present Perfect to talk about experiences.

☐ Using ever and never with the Present Perfect.

☐ Using commas in English.

☐ Talking about the Maori culture.

Unit 7

1. Rewrite the sentences using <u>already</u> or <u>yet</u>. Look at the model.

   a) Have you bought an airplane ticket?

   Have you bought an airplane ticket yet?

   b) Has he found his friend?

   _____

   c) She hasn't arrived.

   _____

   d) I've heard this song three times.

   _____

   e) The play has started.

   _____

2. Write sentences using words from each column.

	1	2	3	4
a)	Your teacher	has / have	already	checked our homework
b)	I	has / have	never	met my relatives at Christmas time
c)	She	has / have	already	seen my mother
d)	Lucy	has / have	never	visited Argentina
e)	His grandparents	has / have	already	traveled to the USA

   a) **Your teacher has already checked our homework.**

   b) _____

   c) _____

   d) _____

   e) _____

3. Match the dialogues to the corresponding pictures.

a)

b)

c)

d)

( ) Have you ever been to Italy?
Yes, I have already been to Pisa twice.

(**a**) Have you ever eaten sushi?
No, I haven't eaten sushi yet.

( ) Have you ever ridden a pony?
No, I haven't.

( ) Have you ever watched a volleyball match?
Yes, I have already watched some matches in my city.

4. Since or for?

a) My brother has had German classes **for** one year.

b) His parents have been married _____ 2001.

c) I've worked as an engineer _____ ten years. I really like my profession.

d) Gabriela has lived in Brazil _____ she was born.

e) Luiza has had ballet classes _____ more than a decade.

f) The geography teacher has tried to talk to you _____ you arrived at school.

113

Unit 8

1. Read each pair of sentences. Use a relative pronoun to combine into one sentence. (whose, which, who, where, when)

   a) Gabriela has a brother. His name's Pedro.
   Gabriela has a brother whose name's Pedro.

   b) The newspaper won a prize. The newspaper discussed friendship.
   _____

   c) My friend is generous. He has a lot of friends.
   _____

   d) That's the library. She works there.
   _____

   e) I remember the day. I met him on this day.
   _____

2. Go back page 85. Answer the questions about Shakespeare.

   a) Where was Shakespeare born?
   He was born in Stratford-upon-Avon.

   b) When was he born?
   _____

   c) Who was his wife? How old was she?
   _____

   d) How many children did they have?
   _____

   e) What was Shakespeare's group of actors called?
   _____

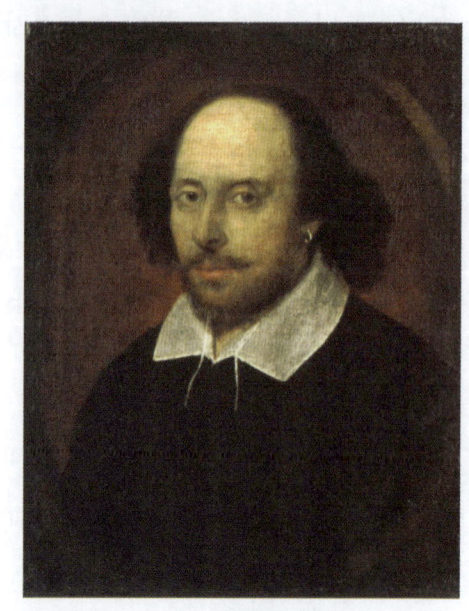

TAYLOR, John. **Willian Shakespeare – O retrato de Chandos**. Cerca de 1610. Óleo sobre tela, 55,2 cm x 43,8 cm. National Portrait Gallery, Londres (Inglaterra).

3. A friend is someone who is… Read the meanings. Write the adjectives.

   a) A person who makes you laugh.
   b) A person who is nice to people he /she doesn't know.
   c) A person who is openly friendly.
   d) A person who understands people's problems.
   e) A person who always tells the truth.
   f) A person who studies and works a lot.
   g) A person who gives and shares things.

   a) F U N N Y
   b) R
   c)
   I
   d)
   E
   N
   e)
   f) D
   g) S

4. Write more four adjectives that in your opinion describe a good friend. Look in the dictionary and describe each adjective.

	ADJECTIVE	MEANING
a		
b		
c		
d		

115

Review — Unit 7/8

LET'S CHECK SOME OTHER PUNCTUATION POINTS:

1. **APOSTROPHE (')**

   a) Use an apostrophe to show possession:
   My friend's house is yellow.

   b) To show that letters or numbers have been omitted:
   doesn't = does not
   let's = let us
   '98 = 1998

   c) Rewrite the expressions using possessive nouns:

   a) The uniform of the player – **the player's uniform**

   b) The habitat of the bear – _____

   c) The games of the children – _____

2. **QUOTATION MARKS (" ")**

   a) Use quotation marks before and after the exact words of a speaker. Use a comma before the quote.
   He said, "I feel tired. I need to rest."

   b) Put the quotation marks and the comma in the correct places.
   The woman said No! This person is lying. It's my dog.
   The teacher said Open your books on page 5 please.

3. **SEMICOLON (;)**

   a) Use a semicolon to join two simple sentences. Ricardo likes to read about engineering; Kazuki prefers to read stories about UFOs.

   b) Add semicolons:
   Gabriela chose Lyndon and Laura Kazuki chose Cate and Sarah.

4. **EXCLAMATION MARK (!)**

   Use the exclamation after strong, emotional statements.
   How nice!   You're kidding!   What a surprise!

5. **QUESTION MARK (?)**

   a) Used in direct questions:
   What's your name?

   b) It's not used in indirect questions.
   He told me what his name was.

6. HYPHEN (-)

a) Use hyphen in compound numbers from twenty-one (21) to ninety-nine (99).

b) When dividing a word at the end of a line:

We talked to them at the begin – ning of the year.

(Remember that dividing words in English is different from Portuguese!)

TWITTER is a micro blogging service that only allows 140 characters per post and it includes punctuation and symbols. Do you have a twitter account?

1. Look at Santa Claus on Twitter:

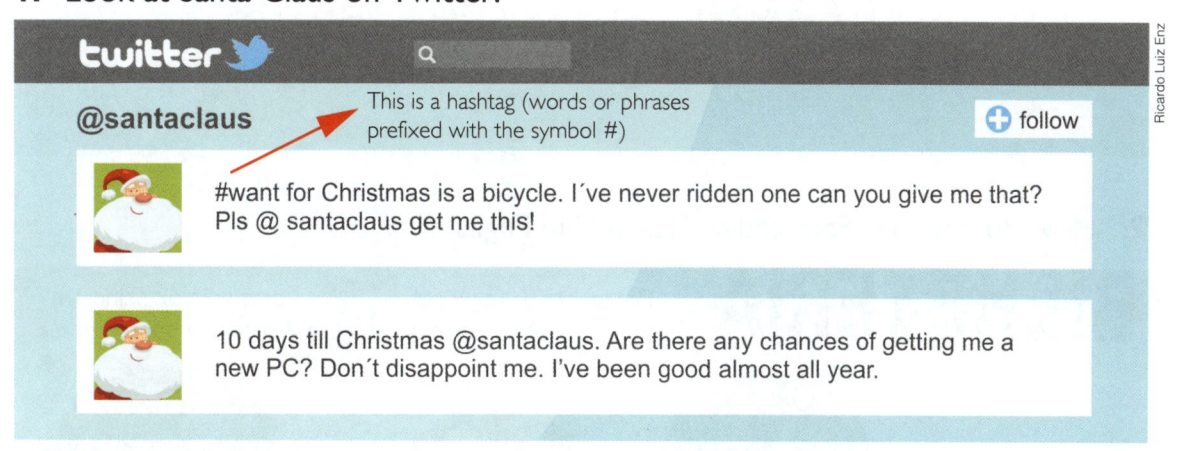

twitter

@santaclaus

This is a hashtag (words or phrases prefixed with the symbol #)

follow

#want for Christmas is a bicycle. I´ve never ridden one can you give me that? Pls @ santaclaus get me this!

10 days till Christmas @santaclaus. Are there any chances of getting me a new PC? Don´t disappoint me. I've been good almost all year.

2. Now it's your turn. Write your "tweet" to Santa Clauss.

Check List – Things I can do in English

☺ I can.   😐 I don't think I can.   ☹ I can't. I want to review.

- Using the Present Perfect with already to talk about something that has happened before now.
- Using the Present Perfect with yet to talk about something that hasn't happened yet.
- Using the Present Perfect with since to show that something started.
- Using the Present Perfect with for to show how long something has lasted.
- Describing my friends.
- Using relative pronouns
- Using proper punctuation.

How do you say… in English?

1. How do you say "mormaço" in English?

   > Gabriela, don't forget to use a sunscreen on hot, cloudy days.

   > OK, mom!

2. How do you say "Faça chuva, faça sol" in English?

   > The weather forecast says it's going to rain on Saturday.

   > Come rain or shine, I'm going to the soccer game.

3. How do you say "pode tirar o cavalinho da chuva" in English?

   > If you think I'm going to give in, you've got another think coming.

4. How do you say "o cachorro é o melhor amigo do homem"?

A man's best friend is his dog.

5. How do you say "sentir-se como peixe fora d'água"?

Come on let's go!

I feel like a fish out of water.

6. How do you say "amigo secreto" em inglês?

Not yet.

Have you bought the present for your Secret Santa yet?

Project 1

FLOOD

1. **What is a flood?**

   According to the Merriam-Webster dictionary, flood is a rising and overflowing of a body of water especially onto normally dry land. It's the most common natural disaster and it can occur anywhere. Flooding can be localized in a particular neighborhood or it can affect entire cities or territories.

2. **How can a flood develop?**

   It can develop over a period of days. When it happens you have time to be prepared to leave your house. But sometimes, flash floods can develop in a matter of minutes.

3. **What do you have to do if there is a flood?**

4. **Read the simulation.**

Listen to the radio or watch TV for information and instruction.	If you have to leave your house or evacuate, take with you only essential items.	Turn off: – Gas – Electricity – Water
Do not walk nor drive in flood water.	If your house is damaged, go to a neighbor's house that is safer.	Try to stay in a safe place. Good luck!

5. **Now it's your turn.**

   Think about another natural disaster.
   - Explain what it consists of.
   - Think about what to do to stay safe.

Project 2

WARM UP: Have you ever traveled by plane?
If yes, where did you go? Did you like it?
If not, would you like to fly?

TRAVELING BY PLANE

1. Do you know what these in-flight safety signs mean?

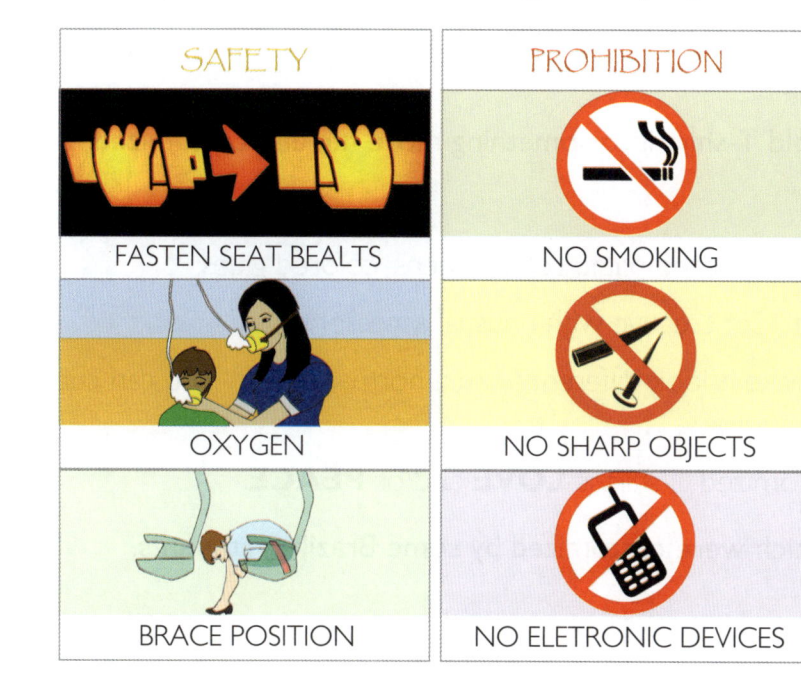

SAFETY	PROHIBITION	INFORMATION
FASTEN SEAT BEALTS	NO SMOKING	EMERGENCY EXIT
OXYGEN	NO SHARP OBJECTS	TOILET
BRACE POSITION	NO ELETRONIC DEVICES	LUGGAGE

2. Write sentences about the signs. Use modal verbs.

   Ex.: You must fasten your seat belts.
   You can't use sharp objects inside the plane.
   An exit row passenger should be able to assist flight attendants.

3. It's your turn now.

   Look for other signs you may find inside airplanes. Look for their meanings and share them with your classmates.

Click

<http://visual.merriam-webster.com/transport-machinery/air-transport.php>. Acesso em: 28 nov. 2011.
Site que apresenta um dicionário visual com terminologia sobre o transporte aéreo.
<www.esl-lab.com/vocab/v-airplane-travel.htm>. Acesso em: 28 nov. 2011.
Site com palavras em inglês relacionadas a viagens de avião. Você pode ouvir e repetir as palavras.

Project 3

CUSTOM T-SHIRTS

WARM-UP: Do you like fashion?

What kind of fashion do you like?

Have you ever customized any clothes?

> How to customize a T-shirt

1. You can transform your old T-shirt into something more fun and customized.

2. What do you need:

   - T-shirts in different colors, colored paint, colored pens, colored glues;
   - Accessorize your T-shirt. Get creative with unusual accessories;
   - Cut, twist and sew to make it look different from a normal T-shirt. You can cut the sleeves off or make a v-neck.
   - The theme of your customized T-shirt is **LOVE** and/or **PEACE**.

3. Look at some T-shirts which were customized by some Brazilian students.

4. Now it's your turn. In groups customize your T-shirts.

Project 4

WARM-UP: How do a man and a woman greet each other in Brazil?

Do they greet each other the same way in other countries?

How do you greet people in different situations in Brazil?

GREETINGS AROUND THE WORLD

Look at how these people greet each other in four different countries:

In Turkey when people meet someone for the first time they shake hands. It's important to shake hands firmly and look the other person in the eye when you greet them.

If you are traveling to Japan, knowing how to bow may be helpful. Bowing is an important custom in Japan. People commonly greet each other by bowing instead of shaking hands.

In Thailand people "wai" when they meet. They put their palms together with fingers pointing upward.

In France people often "air kiss" when they meet people they know. They put their cheeks together and make a kissing sound..

Exchanging ideas

- Which of the greetings seem the most unusual to you?
- Talk to your classmates.

Grammar Points

PRESENT: VERB TO BE		PAST: VERB TO BE	
Subject + be		Subject + be	
I	am / am not	I	was / was not
He /she / it	is / is not	He /she / it	was / was not
We / you / they	are / are not	We / you / they	were / were not

PRESENT

Regular verbs

- Affirmative form of regular verbs
  I / you / we / they   work.
  He / she / it   works.
- Negative of regular and irregular verbs
  Do not = don't
  I / you / we they don't work.
  Does not = doesn't
  He / she / it doesn't work.
- Interrogative of regular and irregular verbs
  Do I / you / we / they work?
  Does he / she / it work?

Irregular verbs

Affirmative verbs
- Verbs ending in ss, sh, ch, x, z and o + es in the 3rd person singular: kisses, washes, watches, fixes, buzzes, goes
- Verbs ending in "y" preceded by consonants remove the "y" and + ies: cry – cries
- Verbs ending in "y" preceded by a vowel: keep the "y" + s: play – plays
- *Have* is irregular:
  I have a car.
  She has a car.

SIMPLE PAST

Regular verbs

- Affirmative
  verb + ed
  I/you/he/she/it worked.
  We/you/they worked.
- Negative
  did not + verb (infinitive)
  I/you/he/she/it didn't work.
  We/you/they didn't work.
- Questions
  Did + subject + verb (infinitive)
  Did I/you/he/she/it work?
  Did we/you/they work?

Irregular verbs

Irregular form of the verb
- Affirmative
  I/you/he/she/it left.
  We/you/they left.
- Negative
  did not + verb (infinitive)
  I/you/he/she/it didn't leave.
  We/you/they didn't leave.
- Questions
  Did + subject + verb (infinitive)
  Did I/you/he/she/it leave?
  Did we/you/they leave?

Comparatives

- One syllable adjectives:
  Tall – taller; big – bigger
- Two syllable adjectives ending in y:
  Happy – happier
- Two or more syllable adjectives:
  Beautiful – more beautiful
- Irregular forms:
  Good – better; bad – worse; far - farther

Superlatives

- One syllable adjectives:
  Tall – the tallest; big – the biggest
- Two syllable adjectives ending in y:
  Happy – the happiest
- Two or more syllable adjectives:
  Beautiful – the most beautiful
- Irregular forms:
  Good – best; bad – the worst; far - farthest

MODAL VERBS

- Ability in the present /past
  Can = I can speak Portuguese.
  Could = I could ride my bike when I was five.
- Ask for permission
  May = May I drink some water?
  Can = You can come now.
- Request
  Can= Can I ask you a favor?
  Could = Could you repeat that please?
- Advice
  Should = You should wear bright colors during the day when you ride your bike.
  Ought = You ought to obey traffic signs.
- Necessity
  Have to = You don't have to pay. It's free.
  Must = You must wear a bike helmet to protect your head.
- Possibility
  May = He may arrive tomorrow.
  Might = He might be at school now.

WILL

You decide something at the moment of speaking.
Examples: I'll fly to São Paulo next week.
My father will call up when he arrives in São Paulo.

WILL								
Affirmative			**Negative**			**Interrogative**		
I You He She It We You They	will	fly to São Paulo next week.	I You He She It We You They	will not / won't	fly to São Paulo next week.	Will	I you he she it we you they	fly to São Paulo next week?

PRESENT PERFECT

Subject + have (not) + Past Participle (verb)
He / she /it has (not) lived here.
I/we/you/they has (not) lived here.

PAST PROGRESSIVE

Subject + have (not) + verb (ing)
I/he/she/it was (not) jumping.
we/you/they were (not) jumping.

WORDS USED WITH PRESENT PERFECT

- Ever / never
  Have you ever seen a camel?
  I have never seen a camel.
- For/since
  She has studied English for two weeks.
  She has studied English since 2005.

- Already/yet
  I have already done my homework.
  We haven't had lunch yet.

Glossary

A

a few: alguns, algumas
a little bit: um pouco de
a lot of: muito(a)
a pair of: um par de, dois, duas
a, an: um(a)
abbreviation: abreviação
ability: habilidade
about: sobre, acerca de
abroad: no exterior
abundant: abudante
abuse: abuso
accent: sotaque
accept: aceitar
acceptable: aceitável
accessible: acessível
accident: acidente
accompany: acompanhar
accomplishment: realização
accuse: acusar
across: ao longo de
act: ato, agir, representar
action: ação
actress: atriz
add: adicionar
address: endereço
adjective: adjetivo
admire: admirar
admission: admissão
ads: abreviadura para *advertisement* (propaganda)
adventure: aventura
adversity: adversidade
advertise: anunciar, fazer propaganda
advertisement: propaganda
advice: conselho
aerosol spray: spray aerosol
affect: afetar
affirmative: afirmativo(a)
African: africano(a)
Afrikaner: a etnia bôer
after: após, depois
afternoon: tarde
again: novamente
against: contra, no sentido contrário
age: idade
ago: atrás
agree: concordar
agreeable: agradável
aid: ajuda, ajudar
ain't: am not / isn't / aren't
airlift: estratégico(a)
airplane: avião
airplane ticket: passagem de avião
airport: aeroporto
alcohol: álcool
alert: alerta
alive: vivo(a)
all: todo(a)
allow: permitir
almost: perto de, quase
alone: sozinho(a)
alphabetical: alfabético(a)
already: já
also: também
alternative: alternativa
aluminum: alumínio
always: sempre
amaze: assombrar
American: americano(a)
among: entre (mais de duas coisas ou pessoas)
ancestor: ancestral
ancient: antigo(a)
another: um(a) outro(a)
answer: responder, resposta
anti-apartheid: antiapartheid
anyone: alguém, ninguém
anything: algo, nada
apartheid: segregação das populações negra e branca veiculada pela política oficial de maioria branca da República da África do Sul no séc. XX.
apartment: apartamento
apostrophe: apóstrofe
appear: aparecer
apple: maçã
application form: formulário de inscrição
apply: aplicar
appropriate: adequado(a)
approximately: aproximadamente
April: abril
architect: arquiteto(a)
Arctic Ocean: Oceano Ártico
argue: discutir
army: exército
around: cerca de
arrive: chegar
art: arte
article: artigo
as: como
as long as: tão... quanto
as well: da mesma forma
as...as: tanto... quanto
Asian: asiático(a)
ask: perguntar, pedir
associate: associar
association: associação
at: em, a
at home: em casa
at least: pelo menos
at school: na escola
at the counter: no balcão
at work: no trabalho
atmosphere: atmosfera
attain: alcançar
attention: atenção
attract: atrair
attraction: atração
auditory: auditivo
August: agosto
aunt: tia
Austalian: australiano, australiana
authority: autoridade
available: disponível
average height: altura média
average: média
avoid: evitar
awake: acordar
award: prêmio
awesome: impressionante
awful: horrível
axis: eixo

B

baboon: macaco babuíno
backyard: quintal
bad: mau, ruim
bake: assar
ballad: balada
balloon: balão
banning: proibição
baobab: baobá
barbecue: churrasco
barehand: com as próprias mãos
bark: casca (de árvore)
bark: latir
barn: celeiro
barren: árido(a)
baseball: beisebol
basket: cesta
bat: morcego
be: ser, estar
be able: ser apto(a)
be about: trata-se de
be acquitted: ser absolvido(a)
be arrested: ser preso(a)
be awarded: ser premiado(a)
be back: voltar
be banned: ser banido(a)
be brought: ser trazido(a)
be in charge of: ser responsável por
be incarcerated: ser encarcerado(a)
be like: parecer
be out: não estar (em casa)
be over: terminar
be sentenced: ser condenado(a)
be willing: estar disposto(a)
beach: praia
bear: urso
beautiful: bonito(a)
beauty: beleza
because of: por causa de
because: porque
become: tornar-se
bed: cama
bedroom: quarto
bee: abelha
beer: cerveja
before: antes
begin: começar
beginning: início
believe: acreditar

bell: campanha
belong: pertencer
below: abaixo
beneath: abaixo de
benefit: benefício
besides: além de
between: entre (duas coisas / pessoas)
bicycle lane: ciclovia
bike: bicicleta
billion: bilhão
bin: lata de lixo
biodiversity: biodiversidade
biological: biológico(a)
biography: biografia
biologist: biólogo(a)
biology: biologia
bird: tipo de pássaro
birthday: aniversário
bite: mordida
black leader: líder negro
blizzard: nevasca
block: quadra
blog: diário online (internet)
blood: sangue
blow: soprar
bluebottle: mosca varejeira
board: quadro
boat: barco
body: corpo
book: livro
both: ambos(as)
bottle: garrafa, frasco
boy: menino
branch: galho de árvore
brave: corajoso(a)
Brazil: Brasil
Brazilian: brasileiro(a)
bread: pão
break: quebrar
breakfast: café da manhã
brief: breve
bright: brilhante
brilliant: brilhante
bring: trazer
Britain: Grã-Bretanha
British: britânico(a)
brochure: folheto
brother: irmão
brown: marrom
browse: passar por
brush: escova
build: construir
building: prédio
bullying: comportamento agressivo
bungee-jump: salto com corda elástica
bury: sepultar
burn: queimar
bus: ônibus

business: negócios
business man: homem de negócios
business people: pessoas de negócios
busy: ocupado(a)
but: apenas, mas
butter: manteiga
buy: comprar
by: através, por

C ➜

cake: bolo
call: chamar
call up: telefonar
campaign: campanha
can: poder
candle holder: candelabro
candle: vela
canyon: desfiladeiro
cap: boné
cape: cabo
car: carro
car pool: transporte solidário
carbon dioxide: dióxido de carbono
carbon emission: emissão de carbono
carefully: cuidadosamente
carry: carregar
case: caso
casing: invólucro
cat: gato
caterpillar: lagarta
cattle: gado
cause: provocar
celebrate: celebrar
celebration: celebração
cellphone: telefone celular
cement: cimento
center/centre: centro
centigrade: centígrado
century: século
chairperson: presidente
change: mudar, mudança
character: personagem
characteristic: característico(a)
chart: tabela
chat: bate-papo
cheap: barato(a)
cheat: trapacear
check: verificar
cheese: queijo
chlorofluorocarbon: clorofluorocarbono(cfc)
chic: chique
chicken: carne de frango
chief: chefe
child: criança
Chinese: chinês(a), língua chinesa
choice: escolher
chore: tarefa (do dia a dia)
chorus: coro, refrão

Christmas: Natal
circle: circularcircus: circo
citizen: cidadão, cidadã
city: cidade
civic: cívico(a)
civil defense: defesa civil
class: classe
classified ads: classificados
classmate: colega
classroom: sala de aula
clear: claro(a), remover
clear the table: tirar a mesa
clearing: clareira
climate: clima
close: fechar
closer: mais próximo(a)
closing: encerramento
clothes: roupas
cloud: nuvem
cloudy: nublado
clue: pista
coal: carvão
coal mine: mina de carvão
coat: casaco
coffee: café
cold: frio(a)
collect: colecionar
colleague: colega
college: faculdade
collision: colisão
collocation: sequência de palavras
colony: colônia
color: cor
colored: mestiço(a)
column: coluna
comb: pentear
combine: combinar
combustion: combustão
come: vir
come along: chegar
come back: voltar
come from: proceder
come in: entrar
comics: história em quadrinhos
comma: vírgula
common: comum
communicate: comunicar
community: comunidade
comparative: comparativo
compare: comparar
compensation: compensação
competition: competição
complain: queixa, queixar-se
complete: completar
compose: compor
composition: redação
comprehension: compreensão
compromise: comprometer
computer: computador
concern about: dizer respeito
concise: conciso(a)

condition: condição
conduct: conduzir
confident: seguro(a)
conjugate: conjugar
conjunction: conjunção
connect: conectar
consecutive: consecutivo(a)
consider: considerar
considerable: considerável
consist of: consiste de
consistently: consistentemente
contain: conter
content: conteúdo
continue: continuar
contraction: contração
contribute: contribuir
control: controle, controlar
convenient: conveniente
convenience store: loja de conveniências
conversation: conversa
convert: converter
convertible: conversível
cook: cozinhar
cooking time: tempo de cozimento
cookies: bolacha, doces
cool: legal
cooperative: cooperativo(a)
coordinate: coordenar
coordinating conjunctions: conjunções coordenadas
copy: copiar
corner: canto
correct: correto(a)
corresponding: correspondente
cost: custar
could: poderia, podia
counsellor: assessor(a), conselheiro(a)
count: contar
country: país
cover: cobrir, imitar
crack: estalido
crayon: giz de cera
create: criar
creative: criativo(a)
credible: verossímil
crew: equipe de cinema
crop: colheita, colher
cross: cruzar
crossword: palavras cruzadas
crowded: lotado(a)
cry out: gritar
cry: chorar
cup: xícara
curb: meio-fio
currently: atualmente
cut: cortar
cyclone: ciclone

D

daily routine: rotina diária
dairy: usina de leite
damage: danificar
damaged: danificado(a)
dance: dançar
dangerous: perigoso(a)
dangle out: balançar
dark: escuro(a), escuridão
date: data
daughter: filha
day: dia
deadly: mortal
deal: dizer respeito
dear: querido(a)
decade: década
December: dezembro
decide: decidir
declare: declarar
decompose: decompor
decomposition: decomposição
decorate: decorar, ornamentar
dedicate: dedicar
define: definir
definite: definitivo
definition: definição
deforestation: desflorestamento
deforest: desflorestar
degree: grau
delicious: delicioso(a)
demonstrate: demonstrar
department: departamento
dependable: confiável
derive: obter, tirar algo de algo
describe: descrever
description: descrição
desert: deserto
design: projetar
designer: projetista, estilista
desperate: desesperado(a)
destroy: destruir
destruction: destruição
detached: isolado(a), não ligada a outra casa
devasting: devastador(a)
develop: desenvolver
device: dispositivo
dialogue: diálogo
diameter: diâmetro
diarrhea: diarreia
dictionary: dicionário
die: morrer
difference: diferença
different: diferente
difficult: difícil
dig: cavar
dinner: jantar
direct: direto(a)
direction: direção
disabled: inapto(a)
disagree: discordar
disappointed: desapontado(a)
disaster: desastre
discover: descobrir
discuss: discutir
display: expor
distinguish: distinguir
diversity: diversidade
divide: dividir
divisible: divisível
do: fazer
do you ever...? você sempre...?
dock: banco dos réus
doctor: médico(a)
document: documentar
dog: cachorro
dolphin: golfinho
don't miss: não perca
dot: ponto
down: para baixo
downward: para baixo (adjetivo/advérbio)
draw: desenhar
dream: sonhar
dress: vestido
drive: dirigir
driving license: carteira de motorista
drop: cair, deixar cair
drought: terra seca
drug: droga, medicamento
dry: seco(a), secar
dryness: seca
due: devido, mostrar
dump: despejar
duration: duração
during: dividir
duty: dever, obrigação
dye: tinta

E

each: cada
each of: cada um(a)
eagle: águia
early: cedo
earth: Terra, terra
earthquake: terremoto
easy: fácil
east: leste
eastern: oriental
eat: comer
economy: economia
edible: comestível
educate: educar (academicamente)
effect: efeito
effective: efetivo(a)
effort: esforço
egg: ovo
elect: eleger
electric: elétrico(a)
electrical wires: fios elétricos
elegant: elegante
elephant: elefante
elevator: elevador
e-mail: correio eletrônico
emission; emissão
emotional: emocional

empire: império
encouragement: encorajamento
end: extremidade, fim, finalizar
ending: final, terminação
energy: energia
engage: dedicar-se a algo
engine: motor
engineer: engenheiro(a)
engineering: engenharia
England: Inglaterra
English: inglês (a), língua inglesa
enjoy: aproveitar, curtir
enlarge: aumentar
enough: suficiente
enormous: enorme
enter: entrar
entertainer: artista de variedades
environmentalist: ambientalista
environmental: ambiental
equality: igualdade
equator: equador
equipment: equipamento
eruption: erupção
escape: escapar
especially: especialmente
ethical: ético
European: europeu, europeia
evacuate: evacuar
eve: véspera
even: até
evening: noite
event: evento
ever: já
every: cada, todos
everybody: todos, todo mundo
everyday: todo dia
everywhere: toda parte
evidence: evidência
exam: exame
example: exemplo
exchange: trocar, intercâmbio
exciting: emocionante
exclamation mark: ponto de exclamação
executive: executivo
execution: execução
exercise: exercitar
expand: expandir
expecially: especialmente
expect: esperar, supor
expensive: caro (a)
experience: experiência
explanation: explicação
explore: explorar
export: exportação, exportar
expose: expor
extensive: extensivo
extraordinary: extraordinário
extreme: extreme, radical
extroverted: extrovertido(a)
eye: olho

F

face: encarar
fact: fato
factory: fábrica
fair: feira
fall: cair de
false: falso(a)
family: família
famous: famoso(a)
fantastic: fantástico(a)
far: longe
far away from: longe de
far down: mais para baixo
farewell: despedida
farm: fazenda
farmer: fazendeiro(a)
fashion: moda
fashionable: da moda
fast: rápido
father: pai
favorite: favorito(a)
feast: festa
February: fevereiro
fed up: farto(a), cheio(a) de
feel: sentir
feet: pés
fellow: companheiro(a)
female: feminino(a)
fertility: fertilidade
fertilizer: fertilizante
fever: febre
fiber: fibra
field: área, campo
fill: fechar uma fenda
financial: financeiro(a)
find out: descobrir, encontrar
find: encontrar
fine: bem
fingernail: unhas da mão
finish: terminar
fire: incêndio, fogo
first: primeiro(a)
fish: peixe, pescar peixes
fishing: pesca
fishing net: rede de pesca
flap: aba
flash: clarão
flat: apartamento
flat tire: pneu furado
flight: voo
flip-flop: chinelo de dedo
float: bóia, flutuar
flood/flooding: inundação, inundar
flour: farinha de trigo
flower: flor
fluency: fluência
fluorescent: fluorescente
flush: descarga em vaso sanitário
fly: voar

foggy: nevoento
fold: dobrar
follow: seguir
following: seguinte
food: comida
for: para
for instance: por exemplo
force: força
forefinger: indicador
foreign: estrangeiro(a)
foreign language: língua estrangeira
forest: floresta
form: forma
formation: formação
former: primeiro(a)
fortune: fortuna
fossil fuel: combustível
founder: fundador(a)
France: França
free: grátis, livre
freedom: liberdade
freeze: gelar, congelar
French: francês(a), língua francesa
frequent: frequente
Friday: sexta-feira
friend: amigo(a)
friendly: amigável
from: de (procedência)
from one moment to another: de um momento para outro
from...to: de... à...
fruit: fruta
full: completo(a)
full of: cheio(a) de
fun: diversão
funny: engraçado(a)
furthermore: além disso
future: futuro

G

gain: obter, ganhar
gallon: galão
game: jogo
gases: gases
gasoline: gasolina
gather: juntar-se, reunir-se
general: geral
generous: generoso
geography: geografia
German: alemão, alemã, língua alemã
Germany: Alemanha
get: obter, conseguir
get lost: perder-se
get married: casar-se
get out: sair
get ready: ficar pronto(a)
get up: levantar-se
gift: presente
girls'room: banheiro feminino

girth: circunferência
give: dar
give way: dê a preferência
glacier: geleira
glad: estar contente
gladly: com prazer
glass: vidro
global warming: aquecimento global
go: ir
go home: ir para a casa
go on: continuar
go out: sair
go to bed: ir para a cama
goal: gol, objetivo
God: Deus
god: deus(a)
gold: ouro
golden: dourado(a)
golf: golfe
good: bem, bom, boa
good luck: boa sorte
goodwill: boa vontade
gossip: fofoca
government: governo
grades: notas
graduate: graduar-se
grandmother: avó
granite rock: rocha de granito
gravity: gravidade
great: ótimo(a)
green: verde
greenhouse effect: efeito estufa
greenhouse gases: gases estufa
greeting. cumprimento
ground: solo, chão
group: grupo
grow: crescer
growth: crescimento
guess: advinhar
guidebook: guia
gum: resina
gym: ginásio
gymnasium: ginásio

H

habit: hábito
hair: cabelo
ham: presunto
hand in: entregar
handball: handebol
handicapped: portador de necessidades especiais
hanging: pendurado(a)
happen: acontecer, ocorrer
happily: felizmente
happy hour: período após o expediente de trabalho (em um bar, etc.)
hard: difícil

hard-working: trabalhador(a)
harmful: nocivo(a)
hashtag: palavras-chaves antecedidas pelo símbolo "#"
hat: chapéu
have a chat: bater papo
have fun: divertir-se
have to: ter que
he: ele
headlight: farol
headline: manchete de jornal
heal: cicatrizar, sarar
hear from: ter notícia de alguém
hear: ouvir
heavy: pesado(a)
helmet: capacete
help: ajudar
helpful: prestativo
hemisphere: hemisfério
her: a, ela, dela
here: aqui
hi: oi, olá
high: alto(a)
high school: escola de Ensino Médio
hike: caminhada
hill: colina
hillside: encosta
hint: dica
hire: contratar
his: dele
history: história
hit: bater, rebater, golpe
hold: segurar
holiday: feriado
hollow: oco (a)
home: lar, casa
homesick: saudoso de casa, do lar
homestay: estadia em casa de família no estrangeiro
hometown: cidade natal
homework: lição de casa
honest: honesto(a)
honorary: honorário
hood: capô
hope: esperança
hopeful: otimista
hormone: hormônio
horn: buzina
hornbill: tipo de pássaro
hospitality: hospitalidade
hot: quente
hour: hora
house: casa
how: como
how long: por quanto tempo
how much: quanto(a)
how often: com que frequência
human: humano
human being: ser humano

humanitarian: humanitário, humanizador(a)
hundreds of: centenas de
hungry: faminto(a)
hurricane: furacão
hurry: honra
hurt: machucar
hyphen: hífen
length: duração, comprimento

I

I: eu
ice: gelo
ice cream: sorvete
idea: ideia
identification card: carteira de identidade
identify: identificar
if: se
ignorant: ignorante
illuminate: iluminar
imagine: imaginar
immediately: imediatamente
immigrant: imigrante
impact: impacto
impossible: impossível
imprisonment: prisão
in addition to: além de algo
in danger: em perigo
in pairs: em duplas
in progress: em curso
in: em, dentro de
incandescent: incandescente
include: incluir
increase: aumentar
incredible: inacreditável
independent: independente
indestructible: indestrutível
Indian: Indiano(a)
indicate: indicar
indigenous: indígena
indirect: indireto
infinitive: infinitivo
influence: influência
inform: informar
information: informação
insect: inseto
inside out: do aveso
inside: dentro, no(a)
inspire: inspirar
instant messaging: mensagem instantânea
instead of: ao invés de, em vez disso
institution: instituição
instrument: instrumento
interest: interesse
interesting: interessante

interrogative: interrogativo(a)
intersection: interseção, cruzamento
interview: entrevista
into: em, dentro de
invention: invenção
invincible: invencível
invitation: convite
involve: envolver
Ireland: Irlanda
island: ilha
isolate: isolar
issue: assunto, questão
it: ele, ela (objeto / animal), o, a, a ele, a ela
it's your turn: é sua vez
Italian: italiano(a), língua italiana
Italy: Itália
its: dele, dela, seu, sua
itself: ele mesmo, ela mesma

J

jacket: jaqueta
January: janeiro
Japan: Japão
jealous: ciumento (a)
job: trabalho, emprego
join: reunir-se com, juntar
joyful: alegre
juice: suco
July: julho
June: junho
jungle: selva
just-married: recém-casado
just: apenas

K

keep in touch: manter contato
keep: manter
key word: palavra-chave
kill: matar
King Baboon Spider: tipo de tarântula
King fisher: tipo de pássaro
kiwi: fruta, ave típica da Nova Zelândia e neozelandeses descendentes de ingleses e irlandeses
know: saber, conhecer
knowledge: conhecimento

L

lab: laboratório
labor: trabalho
laborer: operário(a)
land: aterrissar, terra
landfill: aterro sanitário
landscape: paisagem
landslide: deslizamento de terra
language: língua
large: grande, extenso
last: durar, último(a)

late: tarde, atrasado
laugh: rir
law: direito (carreira)
lay: colocar, pôr
layer: camada
lead: conduzir
leader: líder
leaf: folha (pl. leaves)
learn: aprender
leave: deixar, sair
legend: lenda
lend: emprestar
less: menos
lesson: lição
let: deixar
letter: carta, letra
level: nível
library: biblioteca
lie: mentir
life: vida (pl. lives)
life imprisonment: prisão perpétua
lifelong: vitalício(a)
lift: levantar
light: luz, acender uma luz
light bulb: lâmpada elétrica
lightning: relâmpago
like: gostar, como (preposição)
limit: limite, limitar
line: linha
link: conexão
linking verb: verbo de ligação
lion: leão
liquid: líquido (a)
list: listar
listen: escutar
litter: espalhar, lixo
little: pouco
live: morar
living things: seres vivos
London: Londres
long: longo(a)
look: olhar
look at: observar
look at yourself: cuidar-se
look for: procurar
look forward: aguardar algo (ansiosamente)
loose: frouxo(a)
lose: perder
lost: perdido(a)
lottery: loteria
love: amar, amor
lovebird: tipo de pássaro
low: baixo(a)
lunch: almoço
lyrics: letra de música

M

madam: madame, senhora
magazine: revista
magic: mágica
magical: mágico(a)
main: principal
mainland: continente
major: especializar-se
make: fazer
make into: transformar
make up: maquiar-se
makeshift: provisório
man: homem
management: administração
manager: gerente
mankind: humanidade
many: muitos(as)
March: março
mark: marca, ponto
marketing: estratégias de mercado
Mars: Marte
marry: casar-se
marvelous: maravilhoso(a)
mass: massa
match: relacionar
matter: material
May: maio
me: me (como objeto)
meal: refeição
mealy bugs: pequenos insetos
mean: querer dizer
meaning: significado
measure: medida, medir
medicine: remédio, medicina
meet: encontrar
melt: derreter
member: membro
memory: memória
men: homens
mention: mencionar
mercury: mercúrio
mercy: piedade
message: mensagem
meter: metro
methane: metano
Mexican: mexicano(a)
might: poder
mile: milha
military: militar
milk: leite
millionaire: milionário(a)
mind: mente
mind map: mapa mental
miner: mineiro(a) (trabalha em minas)
minority: minoria
minute: minuto
miss: perdir, sentir falta
mistake: erro, confundir
mix: misturar, mistura

model: modelo
modern: moderno(a)
modest: modesto(a)
modify: modificar
mom: mãe
Monday: segunda-feira
money: dinheiro(a)
monkey: macaco
monologue: monólogo
month: mês
moon: Lua
more: mais
moreover: além disso
morning: manhã
most of: a maior parte de
moth: mariposa
mother: mãe
motivated: motivado(a)
mountain: montanha
mouthwash: desinfetante bucal
move: mover
movement: movimento
movie: filme
movies: cinema
much: muito(a)
muck: estragado(a)
muck: sujeira
mud: lama
muddy: lamacento(a)
mudslide: deslizamento de lama
murky: turvo(a)
must: dever
my: meu(s), minha(s)

N

name: nome
Namibia: Namíbia
nationality: nacionalidade
native: nativo
natural disaster: desastre natural
natural gas: gás natural
nature: natureza
navy: marinha
nearly: perto de, quase
necessary: necessário
necessity: necessidade
need: necessidade, precisar
negative: negativo(a)
neighbor: vizinho(a)
neighboring: vizinhança
nest: ninho
nervous: nervoso(a)
Netherlands: Holanda
never: nunca
new: novo(a)
New York: Nova York

New Zealand: Nova Zelândia
news: notícias
newspaper: jornal
Newzealander: neozelandês(a)
next: próximo(a)
night: noite
nitrogen: nitrogênio
nitrous oxide: óxido nitroso
no: não
nocturnal: noturno(a)
nonessential: desnecessário
nor: nem
normally: normalmente
north: norte
North America: América do Norte
northern: do norte, setentrional
not only: não apenas
note: recado
notebook: caderno
notice: notar
noun: substantivo
November: novembro
now: agora
nowadays: hoje em dia
number: número
nurse: enfermeira(o)

O

obedient: obediente
obey: obedecer
obligation: obrigação
obligatory: obrigatório(a)
observation: observação
obtain: obter
occur: ocorrer
ocean: oceano
October: outubro
of: de
office: escritório, consultório
often: com frequência
oil: óleo
old: velho (a)
omit: omitir
on: em, sobre, posição ligado(a)
on the left: a esquerda
on the right: a direita
on the way: a caminho de
on vacation: de férias
once: uma vez por
one-way street: rua de mão única
only: somente
on record: registrado(a)
onto: em, sobre, a
open: aberto, abrir
openly: abertamente
opinion: opinião
opposite: contrário em frente de
optimistic: otimista

or: ou
orange: laranja
orbit: orbitar
order: pedido, encomendar
ordinary: comum
organic: orgânico(a)
organization: organização
origin: origem
originally: originalmente
other: outro(a)
otherwise: do contrário
ought to: dever
our: nosso(s), nossa(s)
ourselves: nós mesmos(as)
out of: fora de
outgoing: extrovertido(a)
outside: fora de
over: sobre, por cima de
overcrowded: superlotado
overflow: transbordamento
overthrow: depor
owl: coruja
own: próprio(a)
oxygen: oxigênio
ozone layer: camada de ozônio

P

page: página
pain: dor
pan: panela
pants: calças
paper: papel
paraglide: voo de asa delta
paragraph: parágrafo
parenthetical: entre parênteses
parents: pais
park: estacionar, parque
parrot: papagaio
part: parte
particularly: especialmente
partner: parceiro, sócio
partner school: escola conveniada
partnership: parceria
party: festa, partido
pass: passar
passenger: passageiro(a)
past: passado
pasta: massas (comida)
pattern: padrão
pay: pagamento, pagar
pay attention: prestar atenção
pedestrian: pedestre
penguin: pinguim
people: pessoas
perch on: empoleirar
perform: realizar
period: período
persist: persistir

permission: permissão
persistent: persistente
person: pessoa
personal: pessoal
personality: personalidade
pet: animal de estimação
petroleum: petróleo
phenomenon: fenômeno
phone: telefone
photo: fotografia
phrase: frase
physical education: educação física
physical: físico(a)
picture: figura
pie: torta
pill: pílula
pilgrim: peregrino(a)
pineapple: abacaxi
pioneer: pioneiro(a)
pituitary gland: glândula pituitária
place: colocar, por, lugar
plain: planície
plan: planejar
planet: planeta
plant: planta
plant matter: material de origem vegetal
plantation: plantação
plastic: plástico
plate: prato
play: peça de teatro
player: jogador
playground: área de recreação infantil
playhouse: teatro
pleasant: agradável
please: por favor
plotting: complô
plumbing: encanamento
plunge: mergulhar
playwright: dramaturgo(a)
pocket: bolso
pod: vagem
point: ponto
poison: veneno
poisonous: venenoso(a)
polar ice caps: calotas polares
policy: política
polite: cortês, educado(a)
political: político(a)
pollution: poluição
pony: pônei
pool: piscina
poor: pobre
pop star: astro
population: população
portion: porção
Portuguese: português(a), língua portuguesa
position: posição

positive: positivo(a)
possession: posse
possibility: possibilidade
possible: possível
post-graduation: pós-graduação
potent: potente
poultry: relativo à carne de aves
powder: pó
power: poder
practice: praticar, prática
precede: preceder
predator: predador
pre-dawn: antes do amanhecer
predict: prever
prediction: previsão
prejudice: preconceito
preparatory: preparatório
prepare: preparar
present: presente
preserve: preservar
president: presidente
press: pressionar
pretend: fingir
previous: anterior
print: imprimir
prison: prisão
prize: prêmio
problem: problema
proceed: prosseguir
process: processo
produce: produzir
product: produto
production: produção
profession: profissão
professor: professor(a) universitário(a)
program: programar, programa
prohibition: proibição
project: projeto
prolong: prolongar
promise: prometer
pronoun: pronome
pronounce: pronunciar
proposal: proposta
prosperity: prosperidade
protect: proteger
psychology: psicologia
public transportation: transporte público
publicity: publicidade
pull: puxar
pull out: retirar
pulp: polpa
punctuation: pontuação
purchase: compra
purpose: objetivo
put: por, colocar
put away: guardar
put on: vestir, calçar

Q

qualify: qualificar
quality: qualidade
question: pergunta
questionable: questionável
questionnaire: questionário
quickly: rapidamente
quotation marks: aspas
quotation: citação

R

rabbit: coelho
racist: racista
radiation: radiação
rain: chuva
rain heavily: chover forte
raincoat: capa de chuva
rainforest: floresta tropical
raise: aumentar, levantar
rapid: rápido(a)
rat: rato(a)
reach: alcançar
read: ler
reader: leitor(a)
ready: preparado(a)
really: realmente
reason: razão
receive: receber
recent: recente
recently: recentemente
recipient: recipiente
recognize: reconhecer
record: gravar, registrar
recycle: reciclar
red: vermelho(a)
reduce: reduzir
refer: referir-se à
reference: referência
reflect: refletir
reflector: refletor
refrigerate: refrigerar
refrigeration: refrigeração
refuge: refúgio, refugiar-se
refuse: recusar
regards: lembranças
region: região
regret: arrepender-se
regretful: lamentável
regularly: regularmente
regulate: regular
regulatory: regulamentar
related to: relacionado(a)
relationship: relação, relacionamento
relative pronoun: pronome relativo
release: liberação, soltar, libertar
relief: alívio, aliviar
religious: religioso(a)
remain: permanecer

remember: lembrar-se (de)
remind: lembrar de algo
remote: remoto
repeat: repetir
replace: substituir
represent: representar
reputation: reputação
request: pedir
research: pesquisa
resident: morador(a)
resistance: resistência
resource: recurso, fonte
respect: respeito, respeitar
respectable: respeitável
respectful: respeitoso(a)
respiration: respiração
responsibility: responsabilidade
rest: descansar
return: retornar
reveal: revelar
review: revisão
revolution: revolução
revolutionary: revolucionário
revolutionise: revolucionar
rhyme: rima
rice: arroz
rich: rico(a)
ride a bike / bicycle: andar de bicicleta
ride a horse: andar a cavalo
right: certo(a)
right-of-way: preferencial
ring: soar (campainha)
ripe fruit: fruta madura
rise: subir
river: rio
road: rua, rodovia
rock concert: concerto de rock
role: papel a ser desempenhado
Rome: Roma
roof: telhado
room: sala
roost: poleiro, empoleirar-se
root: raiz
rope: corda
rotate: girar
rotting: estragado(a)
round: redondo(a)
royal: real (realeza)
ruin: arrumar
rule: regra, governar
rumble: estrondo
rumour: rumor
run: correr
runaway: fuga
rush: apressar-se

S

saddle: selim
safe: seguro(a)
safety: segurança

sail: velejar
salad: salada
salary: salário
sale: venda
salespeople: vendedores
same: mesmo(a)
sand: areia
sandwich: sanduíche
satellite: satélite
Saturday: sábado
sauce: molho
stand: estar de pé, permanecer
savannah: savana
save: salvar
say: dizer
scared: assustado(a)
scene: cena
school break: recreio
science: ciências
science fiction: ficção científica
Scotland: Escócia
scorch: queimar
sea: mar
sea level: nível do mar
seafood: frutos dos mar
search: busca, buscar
season: estação do ano
seasonal: sazonal
seat: assento, banco
second: segundo(a)
sedentary: sedentário(a)
see: ver
seed: semente
seek: buscar, procurar
segregation: segregação
select: escolher
sell: vender
semicolon: ponto e vírgula
semi-detached: geminado(a)
send: enviar
send out: emitir
sentence: frase, oração
separate: separar
separated: separado(a)
September: setembro
sequence: sequência
service: serviço
set off: realçar
set up: organizar
serve: servir
several: vários(as)
severe: severo(a)
shack: cabana
shake: sacudir
shape: forma
share: compartilhar
she: ela
shed: derramar
sheep: ovelha
shelter: refúgio

shoes: sapatos
shore: orla (mar)
short: curto(a), baixo(a)
shorts: shorts, calças curtas
should: deveria
show: mostrar
shower: chuveiro, banho de chuveiro
sick: doente
side: lado
sidewalk: calçada
sign: sinal, sinalizar, assinar
signal: fazer sinal
signalized: sinalizado(a)
signature: assinatura
significant: significante
silly: tolo(a)
simple: simples
since: desde
sincerely yours: atenciosamente
sing: cantar
singer: cantor(a)
single: único(a)
sir: senhor
size: tamanho
ski: esquiar
skill: habilidade
skin: pele
skirt: saia
sky: céu
skydive: paraquedismo
slang: gíria
slave: escravo
sleep: dormir
slick: liso(a) e lustroso(a)
slide: deslizamento, deslizar
slope: ladeira
slow: lento(a)
small: pequeno(a)
smart: esperto(a)
smell: cheiro, cheirar
smoke: fumar
sneaker: tênis
snore: roncar
snowstorm: tempestade de neve
snowy: nevoso(a)
soccer: futebol jogado no Brasil
social-economic: socioeconômico(a)
society: sociedade
socks: meias curtas
so far: até o momento
soil: solo
solar system: sistema solar
some: algum(a), alguns, algumas
something: algo
sometimes: às vezes
son: filho
song: canção
songwriter: compositor(a)
soon: logo
sorrow: tristeza

sort: tipo
sound: soar
soup: sopa
source; fonte
south: sul
South Africa: África do Sul
South African: sul-africano(a)
souvenir: lembrança
space: espaço
Spain: Espanha
Spanish: espanhol(a), língua espanhola
speak: falar (com alguém)
species: espécie
specific: específico(a)
spelling: ortografia
spend: passar (tempo livre, férias)
spicy: picante
spider: aranha
spinach: espinafre
spirit: espírito
spongy: esponjoso(a)
spread: espalhar
spring: primavera
square: quadrado(a)
squirrel: esquilo
stable: haras
stage: passo
stamen: estame
stand: encontrar-se, suportar
standard: padrão
stand-up: levantar
start: começar
state: estado, declarar
statement: declaração
stay: ficar, permanecer
steadily: com firmeza
steering wheel: volante
step: passo
steep: íngreme
stick: grudento(a)
still: ainda
stomach: estômago
stop: parar
store: loja, armazenar
story: história
strange: estranho(a)
strategy: estratégia
street: rua
strength: força
string: cordão
strive: esforçar-se
strong: forte
structure: estrutura
student: aluno(a)
study: estudar
subject: assunto, sujeito
submarine: submarino
submerge: submergir

subtitle: legenda
such as: tal como
sudden: repentino(a)
suddenly: subitamente
suffix: sufixo
suggest: sugerir
suggestion: sugestão
summer: verão
sun: Sol
Sunday: domingo
sunny: ensolarado(a)
sunrise: nascer do sol
sunset: pôr do sol
superlative: superlativo
supermarket: supermercado
superstitious: supersticioso(a)
supply: suprimento
support: dar respaldo
suppose: supor
sure: certo(a)
surf: surfar
surface: superfície
surprise: surpresa
surround: cercar-se
survey: pesquisa
survivor: sobrevivente
susceptible: suscetível
sweater: suéter
sweet: doce
swim: nadar
swollen: inchado(a)
symbol: símbolo
sympathetic: compreensivo(a)
system: sistema

T

take: pegar
text: texto
text messages: mensagens de texto (torpedos)
Thailand: Tailândia
thank: agradecer
thankful: agradecido(a)
that: aquela, aquele, que (pron. relativo)
the: o(s), a(s)
theater: teatro
their: delas, delas
them: os, as
theme: tema
then: então
there: lá
there are: existem
there is: existe, há
thereafter: em seguida
these: esses, essas, estes, estas
they: eles, elas
thicket: matagal
thing: coisa

think: achar, pensar
this: esse, essa, isso
third: terceiro(a)
those: aqueles, aquelas
though: através de, por
thousands of: milhares de
through: através
throw: atirar
throw away: jogar
thumb: polegar
thunder: trovão
Thursday: quinta-feira
ticket: bilhete, passagem
tidy up: arrumar
tie: ligação
time line: linha do tempo
timid: tímido(a)
tired: cansado(a)
title: título
toast: torrada
today: hoje
together: juntos
toilet: vaso sanitário
tomato: tomate
tomorrow: amanhã
tonight: essa noite
tons of: toneladas de
too: também, demais
topic: tópico
torrent: corrente violenta
tourist: turista
town: cidade média ou pequena
traditional: tradicional
traffic: tráfego
traffic light: semáforo
traffic officer: guarda de trânsito
translate: traduzir
translation: tradução
transport: transporte
trash: lixo
travel: viajar
tray: bandeja
treason: ato de traição em relação ao próprio país
treat: tratar
treatment: tratamento
tree: árvore
tremble: tremer
tremendous: enorme
trial: julgamento
triangle: triângulo
tribal: tribo
trip: viagem, excursão
troupe: trupe de artistas
true: verdadeiro(a)
trunk: tronco
trunks: calção de banho
trust: confiar
truth: verdade

try: tentar, experimentar
T-shirt: camiseta
Tuesday: terça-feira
turn: virar, vez
turn down: abaixar o volume
turn left: virar à esquerda
turn off: desligar
turn on: ligar
turn out: tirar
turn right: virar à direita
turn up: virar
twin: gêmeo(a)
type: tipo
typical: típico(a)

U

UFO (unidentified flying object): objeto não identificado
ugly: feio(a)
umbrella: sombrinha
unchanged: inalterado(a)
uncomfortable: desconfortável
under: embaixo, abaixo
underground: subterrâneo(a)
underline: sublinhar
underneath: embaixo de
understand: compreender
unemployment: desemprego
unfold: desdobrar
unforgettable: inesquecível
uniform: uniforme
unit: unidade
universe: universo
university: universidade
unscramble: ordenar
until: até
upon: sob, em
us: nós
USA: Estados Unidos da América
use: uso, usar
used to: costumava
useful: útil
usually: geralmente

V

vacation: férias
valley: vale
value: valor
vanish: desaparecer
variety: variedade
vary: variar
vaulting: abóbada
vegetable: vegetal
vegetarian: vegetariano(a)
vehicle: veículo
velvety: aveludado(a)
Venice: Veneza
verb: verbo
verse: verso
very: muito(a)

victim: vítima
victory: vitória
video conferecing: vídeo conferência
villager: habitante de uma aldeia
violence: violência
violent: violento(a)
visit: visita, visitar
vitamin: vitamina
vocabulary: vocabulário
voice: voz
volcanic: vulcânico
volcano: vulcão
volleyball: voleibol
vulnerable: vulnerável

W

wait: esperar
wake up: acordar
walk: andar
wall: parede
wallet: carteira de dinheiro
want: querer
war: guerra
warm: quente
warm-up: aquecimento
wash: lavar
wash up: lavar louça
waste: resíduo, lixo, gastar
wasteful: esbanjador
watch: relógio de pulso
watch: observar, assistir a
water: água
waterproof: à prova da água
wave: onda
waxy: encerado(a)
way: forma
we: nós
wear: usar roupas
weather: tempo
weather forecast: previsão do tempo
weave: tecer
weaver: tecelão
webpage: página na internet
website: site da internet
Wednesday: quarta-feira
week: semana
weekend: final de semana
weep: chorar
weight: peso
well: bem
weird: esquisito(a)
wet: úmido(a)
wetland: pântano
what: o que, qual
what about: que tal
what about you: e você?
what kind: que tipo
what time: à que horas
when: quando

where: onde
wherever: onde (quer que)
whether: se
which: qual, o / a qual
while: enquanto
white: branco(a)
wholeheartedly: totalmente
whom: quem
whose: cujo(a), de quem
why: por que (pergunta)
widely: muito
widespread: espalhado(a)
wild: selvagem
willdlife: fauna
win: vencer
wind: vento
window: janela
windy: ventoso(a)
wing: asa
winner: vencedor(a)
winter: inverno
wish: desejo, desejar
with: com
within: dentro
without: sem
wonderful: maravilhoso(a)
wood: madeira
wool: lã
word: palavra
work: trabalhar
workshop: oficina
world: mundo
world record: recorde mundial
worldwide: mundial
worry about: preocupar-se
worshipped: render culto a
wreckage: destroços
write: escrever
writer: escritor(a)

X

x-ray: raios-x

Y

year: ano
yellow: amarelo (a)
yes: sim
yesterday: ontem
yet: ainda, ainda não
you: você, vocês
young: jovem
your: seu, sua, seus, suas
your're kidding: você está brincando
youthful: juvenil

Z

Zombie: zumbi

Listening Scripts

Track 1 – Presentation

Track 2 – Unit 1, Read, Exercise 2, page 7
The main greenhouse gases that contribute to an increase in the average global temperature are methane, nitrous oxide, carbon dioxide and chlorofluorocarbons. Where do they come from?
CH_4 Methane: landfills, decomposition of organic matter, combustion of natural gas, coal, and petroleum, cattle farms, rice plantations, wetlands;
N_2O Nitrous Oxide: combustion of fossil fuel and plant matter, use of fertilizers, industrial processes;
CO_2 Carbon Dioxide: respiration of living things, decomposition of plants and animals, forest fires, energy sources used by humans (wood, coal, petroleum, and natural gas), deforestation, cement production;
CFCs Chlorofluorocarbons: refrigeration systems and aerosol sprays.

Track 3 – Unit 1, Listen, Exercise 2, page 8
Mrs. Costa: Today I'm talking about global warming. Students, how is global warming changing our climate?
Ricardo: We know that temperatures are getting higher.
Mrs. Costa: You're right Ricardo. Can you tell me what effect global warming is going to have on the environment?
Gabriela: Yesterday David and I discovered that sea levels are going to rise because the polar ice caps are melting.
David: And it means that a lot of land is going to be flooded. We have to do something, because lots of important towns or cities near the coasts can be flooded.
Mrs. Costa: And what can we do to stop global warming?
Ricardo: There are many things we can do. We have to stop polluting the air.
Gabriela: There are many people cutting down too many trees, especially in the rainforests.
David: Yes, we need to plant more trees and stop people from cutting them down.
Mrs. Costa: Ok, now please, open your science books to page 45 and…

Track 4 – Unit 1, Vocabulary, Exercise 2, page 11
Environmental issues
The greenhouse effect is the warming effect on Earth.
Deforestation is the process of clearing forests.
Flood is an overflow of a body of water especially onto normally dry land.
The ozone layer is the layer of gases that prevents harmful radiation from the sun from reaching the Earth.
Carbon emission is the sending out of poisonous gas when engines burn gasoline.
Drought is a period of dryness especially when prolonged.
Biodiversity is a biological diversity in an environment as indicated by numbers of different species of plants and animals.
Climate is the typical weather conditions in a particular area.

Track 5 – Unit 2, Listen, Exercise 2, page 18
Mrs. Costa: Students, ok, pay attention now…
Gabriela: Kazuki, Ricardo, listen to the teacher…
Mrs. Costa: Well, I have a magazine here and in this magazine there's an article about the changes of the weather. There are two points in the article: yes, the weather is changing and no, the weather isn't changing. I'm going to read some sentences about it, ok?
Students: Yes!
Mrs. Costa: All right. They say that it's sunnier and it's hotter. The temperature is higher than it was a hundred and forty years ago. On the other hand, they say that the changes in the temperature are not new. It's a cycle. Over the years the Earth gets hotter and then it gets colder again.
David: That's pretty interesting!
Mrs. Costa: Another point: here it says that the weather is rainier in some parts of the world and drier in others. In contrast to it, rain is a more difficult problem than temperature. We still don't know how much it rains over the ocean.
Ricardo: What about the oceans?
Mrs. Costa: They say that the ocean is getting higher. In contrast to it, they say that we can't be sure about what is happening in Antarctica and the Arctic Ocean. It's more difficult to predict. Ok, now I want you to write down in your notebooks the things we discussed here.

Track 6 – Unit 2, Vocabulary, Exercise 1, page 21
Julia Akita: I always use my webcam to keep in touch with my friends. They think it's better than the phone because they can all see me and I can see them. It's also more interesting.
Max Martinez: Hi! We use video conferencing at work. It's cheaper than taking a business trip. It's more convenient too. We are always connected to each other.
Elias Simon: Well, I send text messages to my mom and my friends every day. It's easier and more convenient because sometimes people can't talk on the phone.
Talia Blanco: Hello, everybody. I'm a high school student and I usually send e-mails. But I like to write letters as well. I know it's slower than e-mail but letters are more personal. When you use e-mail you get a lot of spam and there isn't anything worse than spam!

Track 7 – Unit 3, Listen, Exercise 1, page 30
Traffic officer: Hi, my name's Paula Lima. You can call me Paula. I'm here today to remind you about how very simple attitudes may prevent pedestrians from having accidents. So, before you cross a street you should always: look for cars; choose the safest routes to walk with the fewest and safest streets to cross; use sidewalks. If there aren't any sidewalks, walk as far from the cars as possible; cross at signalized intersections whenever possible; remember to walk. Do not run across the street; look left, right and left and then

cross the street; finally, if you cross between parked cars, stop at the curb and check to see if the cars are running or if anyone is in the driver's seat.

Track 8 – Unit 3, Grammar points, Exercise 2, page 32
Can
She can speak Chinese. /Can I ask you a favor? /You can come in now.
Could
She could speak Chinese when she was ten./ Could I ask you a favor?/ We could go to the circus.
May
May I come in? / He may arrive tomorrow.
Might
It might rain today.
Must/Have to
I must leave now. / I have to go now.
Mustn't
You mustn't use your cellphone in the classroom.
Should
You should stop smoking. / We should respect our planet.
Ought to
You ought to read that book. It's very interesting.

Track 9, Unit 3, Vocabulary, Exercise 1, page 33
Take time, take a break, take a look, take a trip, take a shower, take a nap, take a course, take a taxi, take a test

Track 10, Unit 4, Listen, Exercise 2 page 40
Number 1: I think I'll get something to drink.
Number 2: I think I'll take my umbrella.
Number 3: I think I'll tidy up my room.
Number 4: I think I'll go to bed.
Number 5: I think I'll go to the supermarket.
Number 6: I think I'll call my parents.

Track 11, Unit 4, Vocabulary, exercise 1, page 43
Turn on, turn off, call up, throw away, put on, take off, make up, hand in, put away

Track 12, Unit 5, Listen, Exercise 1, page 52
When the bell rang this morning, the students were in the classroom. It was 8:30, but Mrs. Costa wasn't there. Mr. Rufino wasn't there either. The students were waiting for Mrs. Weber. Mrs. Anne Weber was their geography teacher. She was from Heidelberg, Germany. At 8:45, Mrs. Weber walked into the classroom. It was very noisy. Gabriela and Sarah were studying. Kazuki and David were talking and laughing. Cate and Ricardo were drawing on the board and Laura was listening to music. When the students saw Mrs. Weber the noise stopped. Mrs. Weber wasn't very friendly. Everyone became quiet. Then the teacher heard a loud, funny sound. She looked around the classroom. Lyndon was snoring! She woke him up and started her class about the Baobab tree.

Track 13, Unit 6, Vocabulary, Exercise 1, page 55
a) At 7:30, my brother and I were watching a volleyball game in the school gym. Our school team was playing really well and we were winning. Suddenly the lights went out and the game finished. We felt disappointed!
b) At 7:30, my family and I were going home. When we arrived we wait for the elevator. We were riding the elevator up to our apartment. Then the lights went out and the elevator stopped. We felt scared because we weren't moving!
c) At 7:30, I was taking a shower at home. The water was warm and I was singing my favorite song. From one moment to another, it was dark. The lights went out and I felt cold!
d) At 7:30, I was studying at home. There was a geography test early in the next morning. I was reading about the Baobab tree and all the magic of the African plain. Suddenly the lights went out and I felt desperate!

Track 14, Unit 6, Read, Exercise 3, page 60
This is Juliana Varela. She lived in Auckland, New Zealand from 2008 to 2011. She used to work as a General Manager for Discovery Education & Travel. She was in charge of taking care of the exchange students that decided to spend six months or one year as high school students.
In this interview, Mrs.Varela talks about some hints about living and studying in New Zealand. Listen to her interview.
Where are you originally from?
I am from Curitiba, Brazil.
How long did you live in New Zealand?
I spent 3 years in New Zealand.
Was it easy meeting people and making friends when you arrived there?
People in New Zealand(NZ) are nice and friendly so it was easy to make new friends. They love happy hour after work and "barbies" during the weekend. (Barbie is the way the kiwis call Barbecue).
What was your job at Discovery Education & Travel?
I used to work as a General Manager and my main duties were:
– Financial and human resources; – Counselor to students during the exchange program in NZ; – Relationship with partner schools; – Responsible for planning and execution of trips to New Zealand and Australia; – Responsible for marketing strategies.
Where did most students come from?
Most of the students were from Brazil, Germany and Spain, but there were always some students from Italy and Mexico as well.
Were there many students coming from Brazil?
There are a lot of students from Brazil in NZ. Brazilians and Kiwis get along very well so I believe that is the reason they choose to go to NZ.
Where did they stay?
There are students all over the country, from KeriKeri (north of North Island) to Dunedin (very south of the South Island). And they always live in homestays,

families prepared to receive students from abroad.
What was their common daily routine at schools?
In New Zealand, school starts at 8:30 and finishes at 3:30, after that they usually practice some sport and go home around 6:30. Dinner in NZ is the main meal and it is around 19h, after that they have some time with the family and they go to bed around 22h, much earlier than the Brazilians.
What were the students' most frequent complaints?
Usually complaints happened in the beginning of the program when the students are homesick, missing family and friends and when they have to accept the new way of living in a different country and a new language. After one or two months when the students are feeling at home, the problem is when they have to go home, because they really love the program and always want to stay longer.
Tell me three words that best describe your experience in New Zealand.
Exciting. Unforgettable. Extreme.

Track 15 – Unit 6, Listen, Exercise 1, page 62
Gabriela: David, look!
David: What is it, Gabriela?
Gabriela: It's an airplane ticket. I'm going to New Zealand on a student exchange program.
David: That's cool! When are you going?
Gabriela: Next year. I'll be there for one term.
David: Have you ever been to New Zealand?
Gabriela: No, I haven't. I've never been out of Brazil.
David: Who are you going with?
Gabriela: I'm going with a group of Brazilian students.
David: How do you feel?
Gabriela: I feel excited!.
David: I'm glad you're going to New Zealand.
Gabriela: Me too. It will be a wonderful experience.

Track 16 – Unit 6, Speak, Exercise 1, page 63
Eaten sushi; seen a penguin; been to São Paulo; baked cookies; gone fishing; flown in a balloon; slept in a tent; cheated on a test.

Track 17 – Unit 6, Grammar points, Exercise 2, page 64
Eat, ate, eaten; sleep, slept, slept; see, saw, seen; cheat, cheated, cheated; be, was, were, been; have, had, had; bake, baked, baked; use, used, used; go, went, gone; speak, spoke, spoken; fly, flew, flown; write, wrote, written

Track 18 – Unit 7, Listen, Exercise 1, page 74
Ricardo: Hi, Gabriela. I knew your parents were having a new house built.
Gabriela: That's right. They have dreamed of having their own house built since they were just married.
Ricardo: What kind of house are they having built?
Gabriela: They chose a detached house.
Ricardo: What kind of house is it?
Gabriela: It's a house that stands alone. It doesn't share a common wall.
Ricardo: Oh, I see. When did your parents start having it built?
Gabriela: They have worked on the house for about one year. It's a slow process, but my aunt Lúcia, do you remember her? She's an architect and she has helped them on the weekends on the project.
Ricardo: So, have they reached the roof yet?
Gabriela: No, they haven't done the roof yet. But they have already done the floors, doors and windows. It's beginning to look like a real house now!
Ricardo: And, as I can see, you look excited about the new house, the project…By the way, would you like to be an architect like your aunt in the future?
Gabriela: You got it! It's a fantastic profession.
Ricardo: It is. But remember that you have to study hard and be prepared for the work market.
Gabriela: I know it. That's why I'm going to New Zealand. An international experience is a must in any curriculum vitae nowadays.

Track 19 – Unit 7, Write, Exercise 5, page 78
Positivizers
  A. Advise and advocate rather than admonish.
  B. Be a peaceful bridge between Brazilians.
  C. Contribute to a culture of compassion.
  D. Defend democracy with determination.
  E. Express empathy and encouragement.
  F. Foster freedom and friendship.
  G. Generate goodness and generosity.
  H. Honor humanism and humanitarianism.
  I. Inspire interdependence and integration.
  J. Join the family of justice joyfully.
  K. Keep kindling your kindness to others.
  L. Let love be your light.
  M. Maximize mediation and meditation.
  N. Nourish and nurture non-violence.
  O. Opt for an original and optimistic vocabulary.
  P. Prepare yourself as a peace patriot.
  R. Respect and reassure, for reconciliation.
  S. Support and sustain solidarity.
  T. Teach in a spirit of tact and tolerance.
  U. Upgrade universal feelings of unity.
  W. Weigh your words wisely.

Track 20 – Unit 8, Listen, Exercise 2, page 84
Mrs. Costa: I would like to suggest a few tips when you create or design a website.
Number 1: Design a mind map about Shakespeare. Write down as many ideas as you can about the website you want to create;
Number 2: Next, do some research about the resources that might be available to support your ideas;
Number 3: Try to write short, concise paragraphs;
Number 4: Try to limit each section of the website to two pages of A4;
Number 5: Include resources besides the one you are creating so that other students keep on discovering new things about the topic.
Number 6: Start working. Good luck!

Reading is Fun

In Book 7 we saw some festivals in the USA.

In Book 9 we are going to learn about some festivals around the world.

Warm-up: What is a festival?

Do you know any festivals around Brazil?

What about festivals around the world?

FESTIVALS

Festivals are times to celebrate. There are festivals around the world that we can enjoy. When you take part in a festival it's like you are taking part in a story. As most of festivals are repeated each year, every year we have a chance to remember the story and act it out.

Our calendar is full of festivals and there are generally special customs in them. Look at some festivals around the world.

DECEMBER/ JANUARY

Hogmanay

Hogmanay is the name for New Year's Eve in Scotland. In the northern hemisphere it's winter time and the winter nights are very cold and long. It gets dark at around four o'clock and the sun doesn't rise until nine o'clock in the morning. The tradition says that the first stranger to enter in the house in the new year brings luck, but he has to carry a piece of coal. Coal is a symbol of warmth for the next year. Sometimes it can be a piece of biscuit, since it represents food or a bottle of whisky (it symbolizes happiness). If the person is tall, then there will be a lot of luck. The most famous Hogmanay Party is in Edinburgh and it lasts for four days. People come from all parts of the world to participate in this festival. They listen to the bands, dance and sing. You can't miss the fireworks.

MARCH

St. David's Day

It's called Saint David's Day or Dydd Gwyl Dewi as it is known in Welsh. It's the feast day of Saint David. He's the patron saint of Wales and it is celebrated on March 1st every year. This date is dedicated to the death of Saint David. This date was declared a national day of celebration in Wales in the 18th century.

At school students are prepared for the biggest concert of the year and each class rehearses for weeks. They perform the songs, dances and poetry of Wales for each other and their parents. They hear through song, dance or drama the story of Saint David and how he cured the sick and through prayer could make wells spring up where they were needed. In the afternoon most families take an annual photograph that later on is given and sent to relatives around the country.

APRIL

Fool's Day

The first day of April is known as a time for practical jokes and fooling. In the Roman empire, a slave was made ruler for the day during the feast of Saturnalia (It was an ancient Roman religious festival celebrated from December 17 to 23 in honor of Saturn, the youngest of the Titans). Today it is an excuse for small tricks – until midday. If you play a trick after this you are a fool yourself. This day is celebrated in different countries around the world. Sometimes it's called *All Fool's Day*. It's not a national holiday. In France and in Italy children tack paper fish on each other's back as a trick and they shout "April fish"! In Brazil the date is called "Lie Day".

JUNE

Festivities in the month of June in Brazil

These festivities are part of the rich and beautiful Brazilian culture.

June (Junho) is one of the most special months of the year because it the time when Brazilians enjoy typical country food and drink. What are they? Corn-based sweets, popcorn, *quentão* (drink for winter time to warm up the body with spices like ginger, cinnamon and cloves), and other savory dishes.

During this month people celebrate the three June Saints. Who are they?

Saint Antonio – June 13th, Saint John – June 24th and Saint Peter – June 29th. Saint John is thought to be the most fun-loving saint. Saint Antonio is celebrated as the 'marriage saint' and Saint Peter is known as the guardian of the gates to heaven and the protector of widows.

All over Brazil, schools, churches, companies, shopping centers, entities and city halls organize their own events. For the festival to be good, it has to recall the country culture and be held in a space known as "arraial". Tents are put up and typical food and drink are sold.

In this "arraial" there are also bonfires, greased poles and many people dressed in country outfits. This kind of feast is called *Festa Junina*.

Campina Grande (Paraíba) and Caruaru (Pernambuco) are the most famous northeast cities and attracts tourists from all over the country.

JULY

Tanabata Festival

It is celebrated on July 7th (summer in the northern hemisphere) in the evening. It is a Japanese star festival originated from the Chinese Qixi Festival. It celebrates the meeting of the stars Vega and Altair.

There's a legend which says that the Milky Way separates the two lovers and they are allowed to meet only once a year on the seventh day of the seventh lunar month – July. The date of Tanabata varies from region to region in the country and the celebration is held at various days between July and August.

In Japan after supper, families take a cooling bath and then they wear a kimono that is worn in summer, typically after a bath and they step out into the garden. They tie strips of colored paper, cut out paper decorations and origami. Some of these strips of paper have poems or some saying written on them.

AUGUST

Raksha Bandhan

Although Raksha Bandhan is a Hindu festival, it is celebrated by many indians, whathever their religion. It is a festival primarily observed in August, which celebrates the relationship between brothers and sisters. The central ceremony involves the tying of a sacred thread (rakhi) by a sister on her brother's wrist. It symbolizes the sister's love and prayers for her brother's well-being, and the brother's lifelong vow to protect her. It's not just a festival for children. As adults, sisters will give or send a rakhi to their brothers and will take a gift of homemade sweets or cakes. In return a brother will give a gift to his sister; it may be a new sari.

SEPTEMBER OCTOBER

SUCCOT

It's a Jewish harvest holiday celebrated in late September to late October. It is one of the three biblical festivals on which Hebrews were commanded to make a pilgrimage to the Temple in Jerusalem. It culminates in the special day Simchat Torah. It's a time to give thanks for food and friendship, for joy and celebration. The word *succot* means shelter. This holiday lasts seven days. In the first day work is not allowed. Fruit and vegetables are hung from the walls as reminders of harvest.

References

ARATANGY, Lidia Rosenberg. **Adolescentes na era digital**. São Paulo: Benvirá, 2011.

BOWEN, Philippa; CUMINO, Margherita. **Cultural Links. An exploration of the English-speaking world**. Canterbury: Black Cat, 2010.

CARVALHO, Regina Célia de. **Leitura**: Múltiplos Olhares. Campinas: Mercado de Letras, 2005.

CLEARY, Maria. **Talking culture**. Helbling Languages, 2006.

CORBETT, John. **Intercultural Language Activities**. Cambridge: Cambridge University Press, 2010.

EVANS, Linda; BACKUS, Karen; THOMPSON, Mary. **Art Projects from Around the World**. New York: Scholastic, 2006.

FREIRE, Paulo. **Pedagogy of the Oppressed**. New York: Longman, 1989.

GILBERT, Judy B. **Clear Speech**. New York: Cambridge University Press, 1993.

GILL, Simon; CANKOVA, Michaela. **Intercultural activities**. Oxford: OUP, 2008.

GODOY, Sonia M. Baccari de. **English Pronunciation for Brazilians**. Barueri: Disal Editora, 2006.

LAPKOSKI, Graziella Araujo de Oliveira. **Do texto ao sentido**: teoria e prática de leitura em língua inglesa. Curitiba: IBPEX, 2011.

LIEFF, Camilla Dixo; POW, Elizabeth M.; NUNES, Zaina Abdalla. **Descobrindo a pronúncia do Inglês**. São Paulo: Martins Fontes, 2010.

MARCUSCHI, Luiz Antônio. **Os desafios da identificação do gênero textual nas atividades de ensino**: propósitos comunicativos *versus* forma estrutural. III SIGET – Simpósio Internacional de Estudos dos Gêneros Textuais. Universidade Federal de Santa Maria, Santa Maria, 16-18 agosto de 2005.

SAMPEDRO, Ricardo; HILLYARD, Susan. **Global Issues**. Oxford: Oxford University Press, 2004.

SCHOEMBERG, Irene E. **Focus on Grammar. An Integrated Skills Approach. 3rd Ed**. New York: Pearson Education, 2006.

SCHOLES, Jack. **Break the branch?** São Paulo: Disal Editora, 2008.

_____. **Why do we say that?** São Paulo: Elsevier Editora, 2009.

SCHUMACHER, Cristina; WHITE, Philip de Lacy; ZANETTINI, Marta. **Guia de Pronúncia do Inglês para Brasileiros**. São Paulo: Elsevier Editora Ltda, 2002.

SECRETARIA DE EDUCAÇÃO FUNDAMENTAL. Língua Estrangeira, Parâmetros Curriculares Nacionais. Brasília, DF: Ministério da Educação, 1998.

SOUZA, Adriana Grade Fiori Souza; ABSY, Conceição A.; COSTA, Gisele Cilli da; MELLO, Leonilde Favoreto de. **Leitura em Língua Inglesa**. Barueri: Disal Editora, 2005.

UNDERHILL, A. **Sound foundations**: Living phonology. Oxford: Heinemann English Language Teaching, 1994.

VYGOTSKY, Lev Semionovitch. **A formação social da mente**. São Paulo: Martins Fontes, 1989b.

_____. **Pensamento e Linguagem**. São Paulo: Martins Fontes Editora, 1991.

WALESKO, Angela Maria Hoffmann. **Compreensão oral em língua inglesa**. Curitiba: IBPEX, 2010.

ZIMMER, Márcia; SILVEIRA, Rosane; ALVES, Ubiratã Kickhöfel. **Pronunciation Instruction for Brazilians**. Newcastle upon Tyne: Cambridge Scholars Publishing, 2009.

DICTIONARIES

Collins Cobuild Advanced Learner's English Dictionary, Fourth Edition, Glasgow: HarperCollins Publishers, 2005.

The Merriam-Webster Collegiate Dictionary Eleventh Edition, 2007

The Merriam-Webster Dictionary of Quotations. Merriam-Webster, INC., Publishers Springfield, Massachusetts, 1992.

The Penguin Dictionary of Language. David Crystal, 1999.

Oxford Concise Dictionary of Linguistics. P.H.Matthews, 2005.

Oxford Guide to British and American Culture, 2000.

Oxford Advanced Learner's Dictionary, 7th Edition. Oxford: OUP, 2005.

The Wordsworth Dictionary of British History. J. P. Kenyon, 1994.